AN INTERVIEW
WITH IT

An Interview With It

With It

Kahane Lynes

To order additional copies of this book, contact:
Xlibris
1-888-795-4274
www.Xlibris.com
Orders@Xlibris.com
797276

INTRODUCTION

An interview with it is a story about black whispers about our poor conditions and black sufferings all across the globe. The questions they want answers to but no one can provide; knowing in your heart the answers, but wanting assurance; that's what's really happening. The things on the tip of your tongue, but you can't get out.

ANDREW: First things first. Who are you, and why do I have the pleasure of speaking to you?

IT: My name is I Am, but you can refer to me as It.

ANDREW: That makes no sense. "I Am"? "It"? People rationalize what they can make sense out of. Your name alone creates confusion.

IT: Well, Andrew, I am older than language and time, so there are no words that can even come close to describing who I truly am; I won't waste time on that phrase. I'm here speaking to you because you summoned me.

ANDREW: What do you mean I *summoned* you? I haven't called anyone or anything.

IT: You didn't call me physically, but your mind reached a high enough level of consciousness that you called me without even knowing you did.

ANDREW: Wow—is that a good thing?

IT: Yes, it is. You are only the third child whom I have visited.

ANDREW: Why do you refer to me as a child?

IT: I'm not here to answer unimportant questions. I'm only here to tie together the missing pieces so you can ascend to a greater existence.

ANDREW: Okay, well, how often do you visit people?

IT: When I'm summoned. I have already explained the process, but the last time was in 1979, and it was by the person you refer to as Bob Marley.

ANDREW: Wow! That was forty years ago! Who was the first?

IT: The one you call Horus in Ancient Kemet.

ANDREW: Can I ask you for your age?

IT: I gave you my age already. My age is I Am; I existed before time itself was documented, so it can't be translated in your language. Now, you're as ancient as I am. No matter how many times you incarnate in this

place, there is always going to be some residue left over from your original form.

ANDREW: What's my original form?

IT: Your original form is I Am.

ANDREW: What did you mean when you said *residue*?

IT: Knowledge and powers are still inside you and your race. Also, *race* is not a good word; it's a new word, and your existence began before words. Forgive me for some of the words I will use. It's hard to explain with language things that existed before language. The purpose of language is to block your mental capabilities and deny your access to your true self and potential.

ANDREW: Deep down, I've had this suspicion all my life.

IT: It's not a suspicion. It's your soul explaining it to you.

ANDREW: Do you have the answers to all questions?

IT: I am the key.

ANDREW: Well, my first question is, who am I? Since I was a little child, I've always wanted to know that because I knew that I was different.

IT: Well, Andrew, I already gave you that answer. You are I Am.

ANDREW: Well, It, let me rephrase that question. Who am I in my current form?

IT: In your current form, you were chosen to deliver a message to your people.

ANDREW: I'm at the stage where I don't believe in my people anymore, so why would I even want to waste my time on that?

IT: Let me get this straight right now. I'm talking to your heart and your soul, so quit the bullshit.

ANDREW: Okay. I'm sorry. I'll be straight for the rest of the way. My next question is, how did black people fall from being gods to such a low level currently?

IT: Well, as a race of people who not only created the universe and life itself but also accomplished everything your so-called science can prove, you can imagine that after all that, the only thing left to do was go to sleep.

ANDREW: What is imagination?

IT: Imagination, creativity, and knowledge are all similar. Imagination is remembering things that have already been accomplished.

ANDREW: Who built the pyramids?

IT: What's the importance of that question?

Andrew: It's important because, to this day, science cannot explain or duplicate their construction with modern technology.

It: I know what you're talking about, but you have to be clear.

Andrew: The real question is, how were the Egyptian pyramids built? Excuse me for not being clear.

It: The pyramids were not a physical construction; they were a mentally constructed gift that fell to the earth with literature showing you how to get back to I Am.

Andrew: That makes a lot more sense than all the other explanations I've heard.

It: Now, Andrew, I have a question for you. How much did you pay for the telephone you have?

Andrew: About a thousand dollars.

It: How long did it take you to make enough money to pay for it?

Andrew: It's one week's worth of pay for me.

It: Who's the creator of that phone, and what's its name?

Andrew: It's an iPhone, and the creator is the company Apple.

It: Is it a good phone?

Andrew: It's a great phone. It's probably the best phone on the market.

It: What makes it so great?

Andrew: The technology.

It: That's the answer I wanted to hear from you. The problem with your race is that you let people sell you your brain functions as technology because you don't want to use the natural gifts you were born with. There is no technology in existence that is not a part of your brain functions.

Andrew: Next question. Who is God?

It: Currently, God is the white man who has no soul.

Andrew: Are you kidding me?

It: How could the most evil race ever created be God? First of all, that's your creation. Second of all, he has studied and understood all of the ancient texts left by you *for* you and understands that his existence in physical form is to be God. He refuses to obey his own texts and has chosen to live as God. So as a god, he's going to rule as he sees fit. The fact that you don't agree with it doesn't mean that it's wrong. As a god, he can rule as he wants to. If that means the extermination of lesser gods, then that's his choice.

Andrew: This is not what I expected.

IT: I am not here to give you what you expect. I am here to let you know how it works. Who did you think God was?

ANDREW: I thought it was a great being who was going to come back and destroy all the evil that exists on this earth.

IT: First if all, it's *gods*, and why would the god who is lesser than you come back and clean up a mess that the higher gods created? Even with your logic, that doesn't make sense. Infants don't clean up after their parents; the parents clean up for themselves. The problem is your refusal to become yourselves. Submission is what you've chosen, so submission it shall be. It's not his doing; it's yours. I'm going to give you a list of names: Bob Marley, Jimi Hendrix, Malcolm X, Michael Jordan, Reggie White, Bruce Lee, Dick Gregory, Marcus Garvey, Tiger Woods, Mike Tyson, and Barry Bonds. What do these names mean to you?

ANDREW: Well, they are some of the greatest people in their fields of work, but I'm curious about why you didn't include the civil rights leader who had a dream on that list. He is probably greater than them all!

IT: Really? Why is that?

ANDREW: Well, he made life better for blacks, Jews, and women by ending segregation.

IT: So if that was accomplished, why are you still waiting for God to save your people?

ANDREW: I don't know—I didn't look at it that way.

IT: Question for you: do you consistently associate with white people?

ANDREW: On some occasions, yes.

IT: What do they think of the black president?

ANDREW: They hate him, and they view him as the worst thing that ever happened to America.

IT: What color is he?

ANDREW: Black.

IT: How do whites view the *I Have a Dream* guy?

ANDREW: Well, he's viewed as a great liberator and one of the greatest men in history.

IT: What color is he?

ANDREW: Black.

IT: Does that compute?

ANDREW: Yes, it does.

IT: So by your logic, race is not an issue?

ANDREW: No, that's not what I'm trying to say. Race is an issue, but that doesn't take away from his greatness.

IT: Let me explain something to you. The white man will never like you. His feelings about the black president is your reality. The reason he feels that way about the *I Have a Dream* guy is because he saved the white race from extermination.

ANDREW: What do you mean by that?

IT: Well, that was the plan. He was a government agent.

ANDREW: You're kidding.

IT: He was a government agent, and his agenda was to save the white race from extinction.

ANDREW: So that was the point in history when we could have defeated them?

IT: Yes. That was the last great awakening for black people. You had the Black Panthers, the Nation of Islam, and Marcus Garvey—three separate factions, but the three created one mind. Once black minds come together as one, the god force erupts—well, the god of destruction—and it was getting ready to be released on the white race. They all would have been destroyed, so they sent in the black agent to calm black minds and tell them that he would get it done nonviolently. When you had the whites on the ropes, you chose the agent, not common sense. His job was to keep the god force from being released upon them and to destroy the black community and black togetherness. White people can't allow black minds to come together because they don't want you to know your true powers. They are gods, but they are gods through technology. Whatever you can do naturally, they have invented technology to duplicate. That's part of why they hate your race so much. If they had your power, they would not only challenge you but also seek destruction of the creator.

ANDREW: It, what you just told me felt like an arrow through my heart! This man has been revealed, and now I'm being told that he was a lie!

IT: Yes, a great white lie. The mistake being made by your race is that gods are "divine and peaceful." Those are words that were created after existence. Those words don't apply. Gods destroy. Just watch them in action. That's what gods do. Now, Andrew, the names I gave you—what else do they have in common?

ANDREW: I really don't know. After that revelation, I'm lost.

IT: Well, what all those people have in common is that they made it to the god level in physical form. If you just paid attention to their speeches

or performances, you would see. That's why they are still revered to this day. Their magic is still alive today, and it can still be used. Next question.

ANDREW: What is black magic?

IT: Give me your answer first.

ANDREW: Well, it's an evil practice.

IT: Stop right there! You are using words to describe things that existed before the white man's language. Those are practices that have to be done once you get trapped in human form to access defined disciplines. It's still inside of you and can still be accessed, but it takes deep meditation to access that frequency. The white man's definition of black magic is based on Africa. He saw black people doing things that his science had no way of explaining. It defied logic, so he told people that black people do magic; so that's where the term *black magic* stems from. Now he has given it a negative stigma so you won't use it, but he practices it in his secret societies. He is trying his best to become greater than you by using your magic. If you and your people refuse to adapt because of some religious belief, you need to become extinct.

ANDREW: It, those are very harsh words.

IT: No, it's reality! That's how it works, and until you figure it out, you will always be back here to die again. That's how it is.

ANDREW: Next question. The list of people who made it to the god level—did they know?

IT: Only two knew. They were Barry Bonds and Michael Jordan. They knew, but they only viewed it on the sports basis. They didn't put together that they were on the course of becoming physical gods. Also, I left Michael Jackson off the list. He also made it to that level, and that's why he was killed.

ANDREW: Next question. What will happen if we all get exterminated?

IT: That will never happen.

ANDREW: Okay, why can't that happen?

IT: Your enemies know you and your powers better than you know yourselves.

ANDREW: Elaborate.

IT: Blacks are the life of the planet. If you get below a certain number, the planet will die, so that's why so many of you are still around. He prefers the strongest because of the magic you possess.

ANDREW: What do you mean by "the magic" we possess?

IT: You should spend more time studying yourselves instead of worrying

about other people. No one has the power to enslave you. Because you are a group of people who don't know what you possess, the enemy has you use your powers to enslave yourselves. It's not his doing. It's being done on a wide scale by each and every one of you, and it's also being passed on to each new generation by their parents and community. This should have been figured out a long time ago. You are your worst enemy.

ANDREW: Next question. Why is the Illuminati trying to kill us and rule the world?

IT: That is a very dumb question.

ANDREW: Why so?

IT: The world has been under their rule since World War II. Who owns all the goods, finance, services, and entertainment?

ANDREW: They do.

IT: Okay. There is your answer. Now I have a question for you, Andrew.

ANDREW: Okay.

IT: What is martial law?

ANDREW: When the government sends in their military to control citizens and the day-to-day functions.

IT: Correct. I'm going to give you a few names: Amazon, Apple, Microsoft, and Facebook. What do they all have in common?

ANDREW: They're all the most popular brands in their fields. Amazon is the website that lets you shop from home; Microsoft is a computer software, video game, and population control company; Facebook is a social media company; and Apple makes iPhones and other communication devices.

IT: Correct. Do you know what they all have in common?

ANDREW: They command everyone's attention.

IT: You are semi-correct. The first thing you need to know is that they are partners with the government. The United States and a majority of their allies portray themselves as democracies. You cannot implement martial law without an uproar from your citizens and the rest of the world condemning you for being a fraud of freedom. That's not good for your image. Also, keep in mind that the powers are afraid of the population. The more it grows, the more fearful they become, so they have partnered with these companies to come up with a creative way to keep everyone at home. They have implemented martial law without anyone even knowing. You are now only allowed to leave the house for work and school. Most of the other services you leave your house for are under government control, like flights, gas, and groceries. You cannot witness the creative crimes

against humanity if you're blind. There are also creative imprisonments occurring without anyone even knowing. This is who you are up against.

ANDREW: Next question. Was Steve Jobs against this, and is that why he was killed? His sudden death was very cryptic.

IT: Andrew, some things have to be tied together on your own. When you begin to question, you will be awakened. Anyway, the Illuminati is an old dialogue to keep you occupied and to keep your magic working for them and not you. The people of your race consume themselves with too much nonsense. When a so-called plot surfaces about what any secret group is trying to do, it's really what they have already tried and not accomplished. You summoned me because you are awakened, but your questions baffle me.

ANDREW: Next question. Why are black athletes, musicians, dancers, and others better than their white counterparts?

IT: What do you think, first?

ANDREW: I think it's genetics. White people have short legs and long torsos, and black people have long legs and short torsos.

IT: Okay, that's what science tells you. A big part of your downfall is that you are made to believe whites and blacks are the same species, but you are two different species—compatible as far as procreation but different. It's similar to dogs; different breeds can mate. It's the same principle. Now, there's a third white species who has no soul. That's the real enemy, and that's who is your god now. The real white race accepts them because they look like them. They don't know that they are an invasive species who looks like them, so they blindly accept them.

ANDREW: That actually makes sense. Next question. Is the Yakub story true?

IT: I will not answer questions when the answer has already been revealed to you. Andrew, do you follow the British royal family?

ANDREW: Not really, but I kind of heard that they only mix with one another.

IT: Okay, well isn't it strange to you that the most recent prince married outside of his species?

ANDREW: Yes, that was out of the blue.

IT: Don't you also think the reason he did it is to save his species because the course of their reproducing with one another had run out?

ANDREW: Wow! Wow! Wow!

IT: Next question.

ANDREW: Well, I've had a revelation that 2012 was a very important year for the black race. What came to me is that whites born then and moving in the future will not be able to successfully reproduce with each other. Is that correct, and is there anything else significant about that date?

IT: Yes. You are correct, but the most important thing that happened was the reelection of President Obama.

ANDREW: Okay, It, my view of him is that he is a mindless puppet put in power by a corrupt system to keep the status quo.

IT: In many ways you are correct, Andrew, but you also have to understand that some puppets have minds and use their minds without their masters' knowledge to get their agendas accomplished. Not all blacks are brain-dead. Some have a true understanding of how the world truly works and operate accordingly.

ANDREW: What did his revelation do? He hasn't done anything for black people.

IT: Well, he was a very important step in your people's liberation. Every country looks at America as the global leader, so when a black president got reelected in America, it broke a spell created 1,150 years ago against white people. The black minds came as one and broke a slavery spell. Even your gods screw it up sometimes. This wasn't their intention, but the deed is done. Now they're scrambling around trying to create that spell again. If it can't be re-created, they will fall from power pretty soon. Andrew, you have to piece the puzzle together. Do you remember that Donald Trump had a very popular TV show?

ANDREW: Yes. I never watched it, but I've seen some clips.

IT: Well, that show is what made him president. With the popularity of the show, the leaders thought he would capture the eyes of the nation, but that didn't happen. How old are you, Andrew?

ANDREW: I'm forty-four.

IT: Do you really care what a seventy-year-old man says?

ANDREW: No.

IT: That's their problem. They thought having someone popular spew his hate would get blacks to create another spell to keep their power going, but it hasn't worked. His audience is seventy years and older. He has been tuned out. Their master plan has been an epic fail. Your main agenda should be keeping them tuned out.

ANDREW: Next question. What's the purpose of stadiums—well, mainly at the pro levels, like football and basketball stadiums? Financially, they

make no sense. A stadium costs $1 billion or more, and it might generate $1 million in profit each year. They will never be able to pay that back before they die or sell the team. Even if the state pays for it, it's not good business.

It: It's not about the business or the game. That's only to occupy the sleeping minds. It's an energy sacrifice to the gods they serve. The reason stadiums are becoming so sophisticated is because people are finding better ways to concentrate that energy to energize their gods even more. Next question.

Andrew: Well, you said that movies are spells. Is that what all movies are for?

It: Yes, but to elaborate more, what color is Jesus in the images you've seen?

Andrew: White.

It: Who are always the heroes in the mega movies?

Andrew: They are usually white.

It: Your Jesus is always depicted as white. The white man is always the hero fighting against dark forces and aliens.

Andrew: Well, that is calculated.

It: If I am the most honorable and I am always the hero saving the world from evil, it gives me free reign to murder any culture I choose to. All I have to do is tell you it's in the name of freedom. That's how it works. That's also why bombs can rain on any country—because the idea has been implanted since you were young that what's being done is for your safety. Your God will never murder. He is too holy. The same movie you watched on the screen is the same movie they play out in real life. They defeat dark forces, which is black people, and illegal aliens, who are also black people.

Andrew: My question is, when will the masses get tired of the same movie? You can't keep being entertained by the same concept over and over.

It: That is real insanity; that's not creativity. It's programming and mind control.

Andrew: Next question. What's the Trump wall for?

It: It's exactly what was revealed to you. It's to keep everyone inside if they decide to start dropping bombs on America. That's the purpose. Mexico is the easiest way out of America, and the wall needs to be built to keep you in, not to keep illegals out. You already knew the answer, but you just needed my verification. The truth is revealed as long as your heart is good, so trust it.

ANDREW: Next question. Does the white man with no soul worship the devil?

IT: No. He worships your money and your ancient gods. His occult practice is to worship the black dieties. The regular white people worship Jesus, not the creator, because that's what they grew up on.

ANDREW: Next question. Whom should black people worship?

IT: I Am.

ANDREW: What?

IT: A better way to put it is no one. You are before physical existence. Words were not invented. Worship is for lesser beings and people.

ANDREW: Next question. And this one is for you, It. Do you have the power to destroy the white man with no soul?

IT: No. You can destroy only what you have created. That's as far as your jurisdiction goes according to universal laws. You have to destroy your own creation.

ANDREW: Next question. Can you destroy people with souls?

IT: Yes.

ANDREW: How long is the process?

IT: Well, you are asking me to explain something about time when time does not exist. The best way to put it is, the time it takes you to think about the question is the time it would take to complete the task.

ANDREW: Next question. Is this world a matrix, or is it real?

IT: That's a loaded question, but the best way I can put it to you is, it's real because you all accept it as being real. So, since you accept it, you have to play it out until the conclusion. That's the only way you can truly ascend.

ANDREW: Next question. What is value?

IT: Value is what you accept; it doesn't exist. The only I Am value is your soul. As you become higher and higher in your consciousness, things lose value. Value is for lesser beings and lesser gods. Earth is at a very low level. That's why value exists. It's like everything else. It only exists if you accept it. Now, Andrew, what are your perceptions of God?

ANDREW: Well, It, I thought God was a great figure who is going to come to Earth from the sky with wings to liberate us from our enemies.

IT: Is that process the same for your people?

ANDREW: Yes.

IT: Do you pay attention to nature, Andrew?

ANDREW: Yes, I do.

IT: It's violent and unforgiving, isn't it?

ANDREW: Yes, it is.

IT: When you step on an ant, do you view it as a crime?

ANDREW: No.

IT: When you chop down a tree, do you view it as murder?

ANDREW: Nope.

IT: So what would make you think a god or gods have the time to deal with this mess you created? It's not logical. You have to clean up your mess. As long as you view your enemy as your equal, he will continue to kick you in the ass. Two different creations can never be equal, and you have to get that in your head. You are two different creations. Actually, three forms of you are dominant. The whites with souls are lesser, and the ones with no souls are the weakest. If you think diplomacy is going to free you and your people, you're a fool. History shows you that everyone who thinks that that's the answer is dead. Most of them were murdered.

ANDREW: Next question. Are we destined to suffer forever?

IT: No. Liberation is closer than you think. Obama has already started the process. Now, Andrew, this one is for you. If the gods did come to save you all, how would you feel?

ANDREW: That would make us all happy. We've been waiting for this for a thousand years!

IT: Did it occur to you that when liberation time comes, whites and blacks would unite together to fight the liberators? Your own alien movies are prepping you for that scenario. You would fight side by side with your enemy to destroy your savior. That's how you all have fallen in human form. The same way you murdered humans from other countries in the name of your enemy for money is the same way you would fight to defend you being enslaved.

ANDREW: Come to think of it, you're right! We really have fallen to the lowest point as a race. It, does hair have a purpose?

IT: Yes, it does. It's one of your most divine attributes. How many senses do you have?

ANDREW: They say about five.

IT: Well, this one can be considered number six. Hair is a universal antenna that picks up information from the sun, winds, rain, earth, and the atmosphere around you. It's also your security alarm. If danger approaches, it alerts you by standing up. It even alerts you when negative energy is around. It should never be cut. It's also one with your brain, so when it's cut, it affects your brain; cutting your hair is trauma on the brain. Did

you also know that it was a government agenda to have all males cut their hair? During the sixties and seventies, their data suggested that hair was the reason for the last great black awakening, so an agenda was put forth to stop it.

ANDREW: Is that why little kids cry when they get their hair cut?

IT: Yes. They unknowingly have an understanding that it's wrong.

ANDREW: Next question. I haven't watched the news or news shows since 2001. Why is that?

IT: That's because of the treatment of black people. They always shine the spotlight on their negativity.

ANDREW: What's their agenda?

IT: All agendas are the same. If you get enough black minds to come together as one to create a spell, it would keep them in power. They trick you to enslave you. The same movie has been played out for over a thousand years. Keep it tuned out, and encourage all blacks to do the same. That's the key to your victory. That's how you take the power away from the current master.

ANDREW: Next question. I've heard of a lot of things that secret societies practice, and one of them is eating people. Is that true?

IT: Yes, but they eat black people's organs—well, fresh raw organs. That's the easiest way to gain black knowledge.

ANDREW: Dammit! These people are evil!

IT: Do you eat fast food, Andrew?

ANDREW: I used to when I was younger, but not so much anymore.

IT: Well, you have eaten humans yourself. Everyone on earth probably has. What do you think is in some hamburgers? It's evil as long as you don't know. You have been participating in rituals along with everyone on earth your whole life. You just didn't know. Rituals are what keeps them in power, but the rituals need black energy to work.

ANDREW: Next question. What do I need to work on?

IT: You need to keep being a student; never become a master. If you pay attention to your own movies, the master always loses to the student. The master loses because he stops learning. The minute you stop learning, the evolution process ceases. Your evolution is the key to solving the reality you live in. This is my question for you, Andrew: Who are your people?

ANDREW: Blacks all over the world.

IT: What other culture are you mixed with Andrew?

ANDREW: Indian. Not American Indian, but Indian from India.

IT: So you are half Indian and half black?

ANDREW: Correct.

IT: Have you ever met an Indian?

ANDREW: Yes.

IT: Did that person look like you?

ANDREW: No.

IT: So why do you think all blacks are your people? Your identification with a color is not logical. You have to identify with similar minds. Most blacks don't even like you and don't identify themselves as your people. Their identities lie within their agendas. Pay attention to history. History has shown you that when it comes to race issues, it is in his best interest to have all of your own kill you. Doing it himself would be a political nightmare. Also, if he would do it publicly, the black minds would come together for a single cause again, and he's too smart to let that happen. It will be written off as blacks can't even get along with themselves. They come together for any cause that benefits them.

ANDREW: Question for you, It. I don't want to call anyone stupid. My question is, why are white people so easily manipulated by the government and the police?

IT: This is a broad question because it also relates to their juries usually finding police officers who murdered unarmed people not guilty. Okay, Andrew, the first thing I'll say is that blacks and whites can never see the world the same way. Whites see the world with the eyes of the rulers of the world, while blacks see the world as victims. People who have been mistreated since their encounter with the white man are victims. So as a white citizen, whatever my government says, why shouldn't I believe it? Whatever they have done or are currently doing, it has them ruining the world. If a police officer kills an unarmed civilian, obviously it's an innocent mistake made while attempting to serve justice. Whites were born into the privilege. They wrote laws everyone has to follow, they own prisons, and they own everything else, so there is no way you can see things similarly.

ANDREW: Next question. As some of the most gifted people on the planet, how come we don't own anything?

IT: That's not what you were planted on this planet for. You still have the mentality that you and the white race are the same. I'll say it again: you are a totally different species altogether. Capitalism is what they are wired for. You are wired to give life to the planet. Blacks are the creators of life on earth. Andrew, do you believe that blacks are gods?

ANDREW: I do, 100 percent.

IT: Let's say there are 500 million blacks on the planet. Do you really think that there were that many gods?

ANDREW: I never really took the time to think about that, but now it actually doesn't make sense.

IT: Exactly. You cannot fight a cause that makes no sense. This world runs on logic. If it has no logic, it won't work. That's part of the reason the black agenda goes nowhere. It isn't logic-based. It's an emotionally based agenda, so it's basically a church. You'd feel good and you'd come back to feel good the next time you meet, but in the bigger picture, everything remains the same.

ANDREW: Next question, and it's an old question. Why don't black people own anything? I'm not talking about the mom-and-pop stores. I'm talking about anything of magnitude.

IT: And I will give you an old answer: the *I Have a Dream* guy. Your people had their own communities with their own economies along with your own businesses. He gave the white people the right to enter your communities and take them over. That's what the agenda was about. It was to destroy the black communities and the black families. It's the same thing—you agree to something without thinking it through. That was the purpose of integration. Get them in your community now, and you're still not welcome in theirs.

ANDREW: Next question. Does time exist?

IT: In the physical way, time does exist.

ANDREW: What is time?

IT: You are.

ANDREW: Elaborate.

IT: I will, but not yet.

ANDREW: Next question. What is fiction?

IT: Fiction doesn't exist. Everything is real. Your mind can only conquer things that are or were in existence. The saying "There's nothing new under the sun" is correct. It's the same concept for inventions and wisdom. No one is smart. What you refer to as technology and inventions are just things we reveal when we choose to. Most of the knowledge is revealed to black people, but you all give it away for free by taking or filling out surveys or comment cards. The purpose of those is to give your ideas away without knowing it. Once it comes into existence, it will hit the person if it was his or her idea. There's a reason why reporters stick a mic in front of

athletes after a competition. That is the easiest way to gather the best ideas. Competition is played out in another realm, but it's just visible. I really don't want to elaborate any more on this because it will bring up useless questions that I really don't want to entertain. Next question, Andrew.

ANDREW: Why are so few people conscious, or why do so few come into consciousness?

IT: The gods are always awake or will be awoken. The awakened ones are from a royal bloodline; the sleeping ones are not. Now, the sleeping ones are very important to earth and its existence. Don't think of them as being useless. Without them, the earth would not exist. Andrew, did you notice that it's hard for blacks all over the world to wake up and get to work on time?

ANDREW: Yes. I just think we're born lazy.

IT: And you're incorrect. We will address that later.

ANDREW: Next question. Should we fear the technology that the white race now possesses, like weapons of mass destruction?

IT: My question is, have you ever seen the weapons of mass destruction?

ANDREW: Not really. I'm just going by what I've heard.

IT: This is a highly aggravating question. I will only answer it because the answer might be of importance to lesser beings than you. The answer is no. Your purpose here is not to worry. It's to live and perform the job you were placed here for. Everything is written. Nothing happens that shouldn't happen. Don't alter your livelihood because of rumors and speculation. That's the effect they want. They want your mind at a certain frequency to perform a certain magic that benefits them. Ignore everything negative; it's staged, and it's staged for blacks. Whites don't possess that strong magic, just residue. So that's why everything is geared toward blacks.

ANDREW: Next question. Can the white race be defeated when so many of my people are sleeping?

IT: The answer is yes. Now, we're talking about the ones in rule. There are millions of blacks who are white and refer to themselves as white, but no, they are black. The reason they pose as whites is just to navigate through this mess without having to justify their existence. So if what you are thinking about is a planet of all blacks, then the answer is no. Now, even if blacks do not wake up, they will still be destroyed. Their downfall will be information and accomplishment. It's the same reason that blacks fail. The difference is in the mental make-up. Their brains are not made to hold the same capacity as the black brain, so their span is shorter. So

eventually, they will fall asleep also. Just view the last two presidents as the result of their dozing off. They may never recover from the damage they took from those two. Moving forward, you will see the missteps increase; the more invincible he becomes in his mind, the shorter time he has left.

Andrew: Next question. Who has more power—black women or black men?

It: It would be black women because they are the creators of life. She is also the one who brings the computer online: that means she programs the infant's mind. That means your job is to make sure that she has the mindset to create the right program. Male chauvinism takes away from that.

Andrew: Next question. Are conscious people linked? The reason I asked is because a revelation will come to me, and when I listen to a few people, they will actually say the same things that were revealed to me.

It: The answer is yes. Now, as you get more advanced, you will receive messages that others are not privileged to, and when you break through, then you will be visited so you can further your journey. You have broken through, and that's why I unveiled ancient mysteries to you.

Andrew: Next question. The things you are revealing to me—are they dangerous?

It: Danger does not exist. What exists is whatever you bring into your reality. Most won't understand, believe, or know what to do with this information. The ones designed for it will approve it because it solves many mysteries.

Andrew: Next question. What is global warming?

It: Nothing. It doesn't exist. It's something made up by your government to complete a military project in Antarctica.

Andrew: Next question. Is the sun 93 million miles away from the earth? I've always had issues with that.

It: You are correct to have issues with that. There is no sun 93 million miles away from earth. The sun you see on earth was created on earth. We will get into that a little later. There is a reason the Egyptians depicted a sun in the back of the head and a reason the Sphinx is facing east.

Andrew: Next question. What's the deal with alien abductions and the experiments they perform on their victims? It's not really an important question.

It: I will answer it with a question to you, Andrew. If your technology is so great that you have the capability of traveling billions of miles through space, would your objective be to examine someone? That would be the

action of something at a lower level than humans. Even human scientists have mastered forms of creation.

ANDREW: You're actually right, It. It doesn't make sense. I had an inclination that it was the government. My next question is, is there artificial intelligence acting as presidents and other world leaders?

IT: Yes. When you watch a movie, they're showing you old technologies. There are also multiple clones of each leader ready to be activated if something happens. They have to protect their agenda at all costs.

ANDREW: My next question is about food. I live in Miami. There might be about a hundred major grocery stores, hundreds of meat markets, and hundreds of restaurants. Then multiply that number across the state of Florida and then the United States as a whole. Are there enough animals in America to fill that demand?

IT: Simple math answers your question.

ANDREW: So what are we consuming?

IT: Technology.

ANDREW: Next question. Is that good or bad for us?

IT: You are the one who determines whether it's good or bad, not the product. The powers that be morals are about money, not health. You have to pay attention to the way the world has been operating for hundreds of years.

ANDREW: Next. I've been in situations in which logic says I was invisible. Is invisibility possible?

IT: Yes. You think you were invisible because you were invisible. The power to become invisible is dominant, but it's one of the easier powers to bring forth. Others are more difficult, but they can also be accessed. Availability to each of the powers is born into different families. It's rare for someone to have access to all of them, but some do. The norm is they are usually separate.

ANDREW: Next question. What is our biggest obstacle?

IT: Language. Language brought negativity, emotions, status, separation, racism, fear, and so on into existence, and all of this has a negative effect on your people. You're trying to adapt to something foreign, and while you're trying to adapt, it is enslaving you physically and mentally.

ANDREW: Next question. Are we mentally ill as a race?

IT: No. The first thing is, you view everyone as being created equally, and that's not true. Each individual is different. Now, if your comparison is to other races, the answer is the selection process. The other races

(especially the upper class) don't procreate just because they like someone. They research their opposites to make sure what they're going to bring into existence has a chance at success. The best way to put it is, view your child as a computer. How do you want that computer to be programmed? Are you going to build a good computer with someone who went to school for four years or with someone who just got out of prison? What will you bring forth? Or are you going to build a computer with two people who graduated college? Which one has a better chance? You can build a race with better choices.

ANDREW: It, what is the true purpose of racism?

IT: The true purpose of racism is to divide and conquer. The white people make up one of the smartest populations are earth, and they are the rulers. Common sense tells you that the majority rules. Their rule is an anomaly. The key of pulling this off is racism. It makes everyone hate one another, and that keeps them from coming together and fighting the white man. Instead of paying attention to them, each culture spends too much time fighting one another. Racism is their most successful weapon. While everyone is fighting one another, they have turned America into a lab, and they are experimenting on citizens. Has anyone even bothered to ask why products that are banned in most of the world are still labeled as safe in America? You also have to realize that this is not just a black experiment. They have to gather intel on all races. They have to know how each product affects each race. If you all only focus on black injustice, you will only see black injustice. If you see the bigger picture, you will see they don't care about anyone. The real whites who have souls are also under attack but don't realize it.

ANDREW: Next question.

IT: Well, before the next question, I have a question for you, Andrew. If you see someone famous in person, what would be your reaction?

ANDREW: I would have no reaction.

IT: And why is that?

ANDREW: Because they are no better than me. Deep down, I actually know I'm better than them.

IT: And your attitude and answer to that question are right on the money. That's what everyone's attitude should be, and that would create something special.

ANDREW: Next question. What is freedom?

IT: Freedom does not exist. Now, if you learn how to change your

reality into your own, you can live an existence without problems. That's the closest you can come to freedom in this created reality.

ANDREW: What is controlling this reality we're in?

IT: You are. You all shouldn't watch or listen to anything for entertainment. Instead, do it as a student. The answers to everything are out there and are always being revealed. The truth cannot be hidden; it always surfaces. You just have to know how to piece it together. Even your enemies give you keys on how to defeat them. You just need to pay attention. I've already given you more information than you have written down, but you just haven't pieced it together in your mind yet.

ANDREW: Next. Are all unions between a man and a woman natural, or are some put together by the gods?

IT: Great question. Some are put together by us to bring forth a child who is going to fulfill a prophecy. Those children are born with special protection. Anyone who tries to harm them will be eliminated.

ANDREW: What do you mean by *eliminated*?

IT: Killed. Your interest has to be protected at all costs until the prophecy has been fulfilled. Once it's fulfilled, the protection disappears.

ANDREW: Next question. What is our greatest weapon?

IT: Language.

ANDREW: Language? Earlier you said it was our curse.

IT: Yes. It's a curse because as a people who were in existence before language, you had to know how to use it properly. It was thrust upon you, and you think you understand it, but you don't. It's like putting a medicine together without instructions. One in a million might be able to accomplish the task, but most won't. Very few understand it correctly. That's why it's currently a disaster for your race.

ANDREW: Why is it so dangerous currently?

IT: Because your race has magical powers and words can articulate that magic, but because it is being used incorrectly, you all are basically using your own magic to condemn yourselves.

ANDREW: Do our enemies know this?

IT: Of course they know. They take time to study you all. Blacks are science. All technology comes from black studies. They know this, so they use certain tricks so you all can trap yourselves.

ANDREW: Next question. What's the life span of a prophecy?

IT: It can be minutes or decades, depending on what it is. The longer

ones are a process because your people are not ready, and sometimes it takes many little prophecies to fulfill one prophecy.

ANDREW: Who makes the prophecies? Is it something that the gods discuss at a round table?

IT: You're using human language to try to come to a conclusion about something nonhuman. Your perception is not how it works. You all make the prophecy, and you have to play it out according to how it was made.

ANDREW: Next. What do you think about religion?

IT: Nothing. I also have to let you know that I also view the conscious groups as religion. If I were to rank them, the conscious groups would reign supreme because they get their information directly from us. Conscious groups are closer to the truth than other religions. Now, that doesn't mean the other groups don't have validity. They do, but it's not the teachings of those groups; it's the belief of the followers, and the belief creates magic. You also need to understand that one group is more righteous than the others, and one group is going to ascend, and the others won't. That's not how it works.

ANDREW: Next question. Some people charge way too much for their speeches, and some charge next to nothing because they do it for the love and liberation of their people. Why is that?

IT: Your question is not worded correctly, but I understand. Neither is right. Let's eliminate the fake ones out of this question. With two good hearts teaching the same lessons and one charging more and one charging less, both sides are correct, but the one who charges more is a little more advanced in his or her thinking because their price is based on the capitalistic society that's in place. That person understands that bills need to be paid and families need to be taken care of, so he or she can perform the job and not be distracted by thoughts of finances while speaking. Speaking should be 100 percent focused, not distracted. The more focused you are, the better you can serve the people.

ANDREW: Next question. Will the white man with no soul be dethroned in my lifetime?

IT: The answer is no. We will get into a little more details later in the conversation.

ANDREW: Next question. Why are blacks so screwed up mentally?

It's by design. Also, white people and those of other ethnicities have magic too. It's not as powerful as black magic, but it still has power when concentrated. Your enemy makes the rest of the world hate you, so they

focus their energy to that cause collectively and put a spell on your people. Also, you have to be aware of subliminal messages. Most of the masses can be mentally controlled. It's not what you hear that's controlling you; it's waves coming from TV shows, cell towers, satellites, smart meters, and cell phones. That's just to name a few. The real conscious people don't fall victim to these plots. That's why the government views you all as a threat.

ANDREW: Next question. What culture has the most spiritual people?

IT: I'll cut to the chase. Black people are close to last on the list. Blacks are even below white cults. They have mastered your teachings and practice the teachings that you are afraid to use because the white man gave it a stigma that you believe.

ANDREW: Next. Were the ancient Egyptians black?

IT: That's a dumb question but a great question—dumb because you are ready know the answer, but great because even though you know, the white man can get you to debate it with him because you don't even believe what your eyes and your own literature confirms. Blacks would choose feeling good over liberation every time. Every time someone gets murdered or an event occurs that demands a protest, the majority of people who show up is made up of good white people. They usually outnumber you for your own liberation. Those are the good white people you want to save, but the black people you want to also save would rather feel good. They don't flock to the truth. They flock to whomever can make them feel good, and they will make it a point to look good also.

ANDREW: Next question. How much power do you possess?

IT: I have the power of I Am.

ANDREW: Do you have the power to destroy the enemy right now?

IT: Yes.

ANDREW: So if I were to ask for that to happen, you'd know my heart is in the right place because you told me I am only your third visitor since the inception of time. Would you grant me that wish?

IT: No!

ANDREW: Why not?

IT: We're not at that point in the conversation yet. I'll explain when the time is right. Keep in mind that other cultures have wishes, and individuals have wishes also. Some wishes are for the destruction of blacks because they fell, and that would make the earth a better place. Their wishes are even more spiritually based than the wishes of you and your people.

ANDREW: Next question. What's the endgame to us conscious people getting revelations?

IT: There is no endgame. It seems like the never-ending story, and it will always be the never-ending story because the information isn't being comprehended properly. It's good theater because it's cutting-edge information, but the interpretation of what it's for is not being applied correctly.

ANDREW: Next question. With billions of people on earth, It, why did you choose me?

IT: I didn't choose you. You chose me. It's your brilliance and your stupidity. As smart as you are, you accept that you know nothing. Also, you choose not to do research because you know the information will corrupt your mind, so that's why you were chosen. It's because of your stupid innocence.

ANDREW: Who am I?

IT: You are the light and a person with the power to enlighten anyone with your secret knowledge. You're someone who has already made the world a better place for many people. Even though you don't care about those things, that's who you are.

ANDREW: Next question. Is karma real?

IT: No. The world is about balance. It's not you doing something good and then doing something bad that evens it out. No, it's that whatever bad or negative things you do will be repaid to you. That's how it works. Sometimes it might not come back to the individual who committed the wrongdoing. It might affect a family member instead. Whatever it takes to pay back the same pain that was inflicted, that's balance; it's a balance of negativity. That's how order is kept.

ANDREW: Is the earth in balance?

IT: No. Earth is out of balance, but it's not at the point where intervention is needed. A lot is self-inflicted imbalance, and it mostly has to do with the black race. As healers and the life of the planet, if you don't wake up and perform the task you were put here for, then you get imbalanced.

ANDREW: Next question. Are we at a stage mentally where we can defeat the white man?

IT: The answer is no. Mentally, you are probably a hundred years away. Right now your minds are at the infancy stage compared to those of other races. You see the brilliance in the black mind and the way it can adapt to

any circumstance and solve any problem put forth, but it's still a sleeping mind. It's a universal computer that's not fully online yet. The conscious sector is placed here to guide and protect the sleeping mind until it wakes up. You're the guardians of your race; that's your purpose. You also have to make sure the body is protected so no harm comes to it.

ANDREW: That's a hundred more years of murders of our race. Can we withstand that?

IT: If you think blacks will be wiped out in one hundred years, you're incorrect, and your enemy knows that also.

ANDREW: Do you know why white people get cancer so much?

IT: They get it from all the tactics they are trying to kill you with. It's not for a lack of trying. They are, but your adaptability to everything they try backfires and kills more of them than you.

ANDREW: Next question. If I could round up 10 million men and women to fight against them, would we stand a chance?

IT: No. Let's say that one week from now, the war is going to start. As the white man, I wouldn't even have to display any troops. All I would have to do is speak to all your followers and offer them money, women, drugs—basically whatever they can imagine. By Saturday, you'd be lucky if you had ten thousand troops ready for battle, and that's not a shot at blacks, but the mind is still asleep. It's like offering kids treats. You will be lucky if the fight lasts two days. After your ten thousand troops are slaughtered, he will go back and terminate the 2,990,000 people he made the deal with. That's how he really operates.

ANDREW: Next question. Was the Million Man March a success?

IT: No, it was a waste of time. The white man knew it, and Minister Farrakhan knew it also. He's the one who is privileged to consciousness. He also gets information. It was great for the economy, a feel good black story, and he put over one million black lives at risk. The march was Farrakhan's ego at play, not black liberation. If it had been about liberation, it would have been the Million Man Meditation, and that could have destroyed your enemy in one day. One million-plus minds coming together for the same agenda is what your enemy fears. That much magic together in one place is the most powerful force in the universe. The white man welcomed you, and you gave him a free stimulus package. If he hadn't welcomed you, he could have dropped bombs on you while you were at prayer, and there would have been nothing you could do. Again, you all always choose the wrong side. You all should have chosen Khalid Muhammad and his

teachings. It would have ousted Farrakhan. Khalid Muhammad's message was true. He wasn't on any white man's payroll. He spoke the truth as it was revealed to him. When primetime TV accepts you and you are willing to share your message, it's because you're on their payroll. It's the same game being played over and over to make them feel good so they can go home and sleep. Farrakhan is more interested in his hair than the black cause. The white man will always accept the light skinned black person rather than the dark skinned black person, and each and every one of you did also.

Andrew: Next question.

It: Wait, the next question is mine, Andrew. If I offered every black person in America the choice between the opportunity to listen to the top ten conscious people with all expenses paid and all the food they wanted and the opportunity to attend a barbecue with the top ten barbecue chefs with all they could eat and all expenses paid, where would the most blacks attend? Now keep in mind, one is about liberation and the other is bullshit. Both have free food, and each venue can accommodate ten million people. Which venue would come close to filling up?

Andrew: The barbecue event would come close to filling up.

It: Would they be close to even or a landslide for the barbecue?

Andrew: A landslide for the barbecue.

It: You don't think the white man knows this? You're dealing with and trying to liberate a sleeping mind.

Andrew: Next question. Should I take the white man's medicines or vaccines?

It: The answer is yes and no. The conspiracy is true. He's trying to kill you and neutralize your powers through vaccines. Now, there are preventive measures; you can take premedication to neutralize its effect and things you can do afterward to accomplish the same. I'll explain to you further but leave it out for your notes. Also, you are medicine. Of whatever you eat, the waste exits through the back and the cure exits through the front. That's how the body works. The body is the greatest chemist on earth. You have to understand your biology. Also, whites and blacks are different. Synthetic drugs help their ailments but harm the black body. If you're afraid of what exits your front, there are many herbs that can cure almost anything. There are people you call witch doctors who can do the same. The real ones who have been practicing ancient medicine rituals for thousands of years are the best ones, so there are many alternatives

available. Now, Andrew, I have another question for you. Has anyone ever overestimated the black race?

ANDREW: What do you mean?

IT: Suppose your race was not placed here for great achievements. What if their achievements are an anomaly? What if what you witness is what it's supposed to be? What if capitalism is not in your DNA and it was bred into the white race?

ANDREW: Isn't that the theory that has legs that needs to be examined?

IT: You're so right.

ANDREW: Damn, that might be it!

IT: Now, I know the answer, but in your quest, you can't leave any stone unturned. You have to get the truth at all costs, even if it's not the answer you or your people want and will accept. You need to stick to the truth. Sometimes the truth is very uncomfortable. The truth also helps and answers for your enemies, but the truth is universal law.

ANDREW: Next question. Are there demons possessing people on Earth?

IT: No. All spirits roaming the earth were people who were once living. There are good spirits and bad spirits. Just open your mind. Suppose you see someone who woke up with claw marks. What if those claw marks were just whip marks from a slave master's spirit? You have to stop believing what people say and start believing your logic. What makes logical sense? A demon scratching you or a slave master hitting you with his whip because he doesn't know he's dead and is still living out his practices?

ANDREW: Next question. Name something that the white man has that we don't have.

IT: Instinct. The white man instinctively knows that you are his enemy. Pay attention to how nature operates. Prey is born with defensive mechanisms that keeps it on alert for predators. Also, pay attention to what happens to the native animals when a predatory animal is introduced. The predatory animal wipes out the native species. You don't have instinct because you have no need to. You were the first ones on this planet, and you had no predators. You were on top of the food chain, and you created the predator. An invasive species is just carrying out the laws of nature; murdering blacks is not. You all see the viciousness toward you, and you ignore it because you just want to be equal. You still have that "Can we all just get along" mentality, which was staged. You all fall for the same things through different processes. Also pay attention to the I Have a Dream guy and Rodney King. That's no coincidence. It's calculated. Remember the

speech "Little black boys will play with little black girls"? Now you see in real life. Your black athletes are now playing with the white girls, so you see the process. You don't view it as them stealing the male lions from the pride. It's DNA theft.

ANDREW: Next question. Name something else that separates us.

IT: Well, identity. If a white man plays basketball, he identifies himself as a white basketball player, and he is proud of it. If a black man plays basketball, he identifies himself as a basketball player. He becomes the job and doesn't even remember his color. A janitor will fight you for his mop because he becomes his job. White people only work their scheduled time, not a minute more. Blacks will do a little extra without pay because they are the job. If you are Muslim, you are not a black Muslim; you're Muslim. If you are a white Christian, you are a white Christian. If you are a black Christian, you are a Christian. Blacks often become what they're into, while whites are always white first; their color unites them. Now, don't get discouraged. Black people's minds are still asleep. Also, you were the first ones here. The white man labeled you all as black with the language he created. His label is a theory. You can't invent a language, label anything that predates that language, and then say it's a fact. It's all theories. Most of his theories are incorrect, and that's why he is always fishing your minds. He is still trying to find the truth, and he is still trying to figure out your mind. The problem is that he's trying to figure out something that is still off line. Once your mind does truly come online, it will destroy him. Also, let me go back to a previous point. A spaceman is not going to travel millions of light years to earth to give white people a checkup. That's your government. That's a creative way of checking how much time the white race has left to reproduce. Just imagine a glass of lemonade. I make a cup, drink half, and then add water. It still tastes like lemonade, just a little less strong. Then I drink another half and then add more water. After each process, I taste less lemon to the point that all that's left is water. Now, apply that to the creation of the white race. As they reproduce, they get weaker and weaker. The ones who refuse to mix with blacks become more and more deformed. Some of them become so deformed that they become aliens. The others who are born with lung, heart, kidney, or liver issues are given organs from murdered black men all over the world as long as they have the money. If you have the ability to travel light years, common sense will tell you that. Before I get to that point, I would have to master human

biology and genetics before I mastered space travel. That's common sense, so why do I need to give you a physical?

ANDREW: Next question. It's hard to even digest that one. What was the reason behind Hitler wanting a superior race with blond hair and blue eyes?

IT: That was about mind control. Just look at it as creating the same robots with the same programming. There is more to the story, but he has little relevance to what I'm trying to accomplish with you. But anyway, people with blond hair and blue eyes are easy to control with subliminal messages. Just think of the phrase "dumb blonde."

ANDREW: Next question. You have mentioned a lot about the magical powers we possess. What are the capabilities of that magic?

IT: Your capabilities are I Am. Everything is possible as long as you focus. Also, it's something you should practice on your own until you master it. Negative thoughts prevent spells from working. For example, suppose you and a friend are working on a spell. You know it's going to work, but he doesn't think it will. He's going through the motions like he believes, but he doesn't. That creates a positive and negative balance because the minds are not in sequence; with equal balance it won't work. There has to be more positive than negative for it to work in a group setting. If you are in a group that's 60 percent positive and 40 percent negative, the magic will work but it won't be as strong. Whites are the masters of this. They create events for your mind to all come together as one to use your magic against you.

ANDREW: Next question. When will we come online?

IT: When you are choose to collectively, but in the meantime, you can protect yourselves by not letting your enemies into your reality. Everything is played out the way you let it play out. You are in control. Stay away from negative thoughts, and be selective with your words because you don't want to create a spell that works against you. Andrew, have you ever driven next to a car and you and the other driver have looked at each other at the same time?

ANDREW: Yes, that has happened on many occasions.

IT: That's just each of you accepting the other into your realities.

ANDREW: Next. What's the worst disease for blacks?

IT: Negativity. That's the most destructive force. That is the force that helps enslave you, and that's the force that keeps the cloud over your reality. It's the life and blood of your enemies. That's the secret to stealing your magic. That's the driving force of religion. It's not to come back because

God loves you, but come back so God doesn't punish you. Negativity rules. You have solved this and that's why your life is the way it is, but too many haven't. That's why most people are still living the same reality over and over. Do you notice that your reality and those of others around you are different?

ANDREW: Yes, I do.

IT: That's because you have broken through, and others haven't. Every time you solve a part of the mystery, it changes a negative part of your reality. People will view you as a fraud because you are not affected by the same struggles they are facing. They just won't grasp the same concept that the only difference is that you have broken through. The next question is for you, Andrew. If I were to say to you that the strongest is the weakest and one day will overthrow his captor, he has magic that he doesn't know how to use, and once he figures it all out, he will prevail and live happily forever, what would you say?

ANDREW: I would say it's a movie.

IT: Just let it sink in. The next question is for you again, Andrew. Do your people research the president's executive orders?

ANDREW: No. They could care less about them.

IT: When the United Nations imposes sanctions on a nation, do you look into what those sanctions are?

ANDREW: No.

IT: Question number three. Who is the most powerful army in the world?

ANDREW: The United States.

IT: Have you done research to gather evidence to see if they are actually the best or if they are simply saying it?

ANDREW: No, I haven't.

IT: How many conflicts is the United States currently involved with around the world now?

ANDREW: I don't know exactly, but it's a few.

IT: Every country with which they are in conflict has had sanctions placed on it, correct?

ANDREW: Yes.

IT: Did it ever occur to you that a part of those sanctions is intended to disarm that country, then after they're disarmed the United States attacks them? Has that ever occurred to you?

ANDREW: No...

IT: So is it a great army as stated, or is it fighting countries whose weapons were taken away by sanctions? You have to piece the puzzle together. That's why your enemy can get away with the same things over and over. Everyone views the gossip as the truth, but no one takes the time to verify. You all only go with what you hear—that's blacks and the good whites also. The good whites and blacks are in the same group. You all are pieces of crap.

ANDREW: Next question. Can you name an incident where we came together as one and used our magic for us and not against us?

IT: Yes. The answer to that would be the O. J. Simpson trial. Now, keep in mind, this was also a government setup. They stacked the deck against him, subliminally and intentionally put suggestions in your minds that he was guilty, and leaked evidence of his guilt, but black magic got him cleaned. It was a victory for black people and a big loss for the government. That made them realize that they have to avoid letting the black minds work as a single unit at all costs. When something is too public and too informational, it's usually staged. This wasn't about a crime; this was to get a gauge on how powerful the magic is. They got their answer, and the answer is a problem.

ANDREW: Can a person win a physical battle against magic? Well, magic that is more powerful than your greatest weapons and that can disarm a nuclear weapon only with thoughts?

IT: Question for you, Andrew. Does it benefit a billionaire to tell you he's a billionaire?

ANDREW: No. A billionaire doesn't care what a regular person thinks, so why would he waste his time?

IT: Now, in that context, would it benefit the government to tell the people how powerful and destructive their weapons are? Doesn't make sense, does it?

ANDREW: No. It doesn't make sense at all.

IT: Now, when they tell people about the power, they are really only talking to black people. They're trying to place in your minds the idea that they have the power to destroy you. They do that because they're afraid of your powers, and they want you to be afraid so you don't use your magic against them. They also know the most powerful minds reside in the United States, and if the United States falls, then the world falls.

ANDREW: With all their threats, why hasn't there been mass murder in America?

It: The reason is that if they do it publicly, once blacks get wind of it, their minds will unite for preservation. That's why nothing has happened yet. They are basically relegated to killing one at a time. Imagine how long it will take to accomplish their goal of wiping you all off the planet. Also, when they say "wiping blacks off the planet," they really mean America. Your minds are further along than those of the rest of the world, so you all have the power to destroy the earth, and I'm talking about a sleeping mind. Once it's fully awoken, whatever capabilities you can imagine will be. Andrew, are you familiar with the movies *I, Robot* and *Terminator?*

Andrew: Yes.

It: Skynet and Spooner are the black mind; once it's fully online, you will have control of everything on the planet. You also have to understand: if something is electric, you will be able to control it also because you all are electrical beings.

Andrew: Next question. When we have conscious seminars and meetings, what should the topics and teachings be?

It: The same things they have always been. The only thing that should be added is that everyone should take at least thirty minutes to meditate. The meditation should be about making the sleeping black mind wake up and not about wishing. You need to make it happen. Wishing makes nothing happen, while making it happen makes it happen. That's how it works.

Andrew: Next question. In college and professional sports around the United States, why does a majority of the teams have black athletes rather than white athletes? Is it because we are much better than the whites?

It: You have to view each subject as a world leader and not as a citizen or a fan. If you have 328 million people living in America, you can find enough capable white people to fill every spot on every sports team. That's a fact. You are basically shipped to those teams for two reasons: one is to grow the black population in that city and state and the other is to control the weather. Controlling the weather is something blacks do naturally without thinking. Also, when you're trying to grow the population, you want the strongest black men to mix with white women.

Andrew: Next question. Should I be concerned about the way our images and character have been assassinated through the news, movies, and media?

It: No. Your concerns shouldn't be about people who hate you. Their magic is weak, so their hate has minimal effect on you. Only spend your

time and energy when you're subjected to an issue. You worry about tomorrow, and tomorrow you worry about your bills on the day they are due, and not the day before. Live every day the best you can worry free. That's the way it's made to work. Don't occupy your time with subjects that are not important for that day.

ANDREW: Next question. If this reality is not real and is just a movie being played out, should we just kill ourselves and enter a new reality?

IT: No. It doesn't work that way. The magic that's running this planet is that blacks wish to see it to the end—the day when the soulless man will be defeated and blacks will live happily ever after. That's what controls the planet as we speak. So now you have no choice but to see it through, so people who choose to kill themselves will be brought back here to continue the story until it ends.

ANDREW: Next question. Is having too many friends a good or bad thing?

IT: Andrew, do you know what the pecking order is?

ANDREW: Yes.

IT: Well, the leader of the pecking order controls that reality, so people who have many friends visit many different realities. Some they control, and some they don't. Everyone's reality isn't good because you really don't know what's in someone's heart. So you can be killed by just visiting someone's reality if it's full of negativity, so too many friends is not a good thing at all. You need to try to always be in realities you create or control. Also, kids' realities are good places to be because they are filled with powerful magic; that's why kids keep you young and happy. It's the magic they create.

ANDREW: Next. What is the real purpose of emojis?

IT: It's conditioning young minds to read ancient hieroglyphics. The white man hasn't solved anything yet. He has told you he has and everyone has accepted his solutions, but he hasn't solved anything and he knows it. So emojis are his creative way of conditioning young minds so someone can rise up and solve them in the future.

ANDREW: Before we continue, I know a lot of people are going to have a lot of questions about you.

IT: Okay, Andrew, give me your best question because I will only answer one. Once we're done, I can answer anything else, but those answers will be for you only.

ANDREW: Okay. My question is, have you ever existed in the physical world?

IT: The answer is no.

ANDREW: Next question. What is the heart chakra?

IT: Great question. My question to you, Andrew, is what's your quest?

ANDREW: My quest is the liberation of my people.

IT: This question doesn't help to liberate your people. This is advanced teaching that is for the conscious community for your protection and helping you all with creating and living in your own realities until everyone comes online. This is the point all conscious people are missing. What's being revealed is not for your people. It's for you and your protection. Everyone can't be dead. If everyone is dead, there will be no resistance. You all are the resistance they talk about in the movies. Most of the mass do not understand your teachings, so they can't become conscious. Even most of your conscious patrons don't want to get through the lectures unless the speaker has comedy in the routine. If there is no comedy, you lose them. That's why it's usually the most popular conscious people who are the most funny. It's not about the teachings. It's about feeling good while learning; that's the sleeping mind. Also, you can't teach college in a first-grade curriculum. You have to teach the first-grade curriculum; you have to teach ABCs and 123s. That's the only way you can wake up the sleeping mind. You have to become a great teacher, and you have to understand your students. Yes, you can sound sophisticated to the conscious community, but you shut down the masses. You push them out. That's why you all have the same question on why they won't wake up. The *why* is you all.

ANDREW: What's one thing we should not do when we are lecturing?

IT: Take questions or answer questions while you are speaking. Get through the lecture, and then you take the questions on an individual basis. The keywords are *individual basis*. You too often fall for the same government tricks—paid distraction. Everyone in the lecture is not a conscious person. Some are government agents sent there to destroy the teachings. You can easily identify them by their questions. They are briefed on what questions to ask, so they will ask you a question about a topic that has nothing to do with the subject you are currently teaching. So, as a good teacher, you take the time out to answer the question and help someone whose mind wants to learn, but you are the one who got tricked and missed the point. The two hours of teachings before the question just got thrown out the door. That's what their agenda was, and it got accomplished.

ANDREW: Next question. Some conscious speakers do better than others financially. If they have extra money, what should they use it for?

IT: Research, and not research on more education because that's provided to you all free from us. It should be spent on checking air quality, water quality, and earth quality. That's how you can get more people interested. Black churches should also do the same. Even the most dead person cares about his or her health more than education. Spend a day at the farmers market, and you will see what the sleeping black mind is about. That's what you all need to add to your speeches, and you will wake up more minds. Even the most dead person knows the government is trying to kill him or her.

ANDREW: Next question. During televised sporting events, what's the purpose of the announcers? Why do I need someone to tell me what I'm looking at?

IT: You also need to include point spreads, debate shows, and pregame shows in this question because they're all together. This is how black magic works. This is for black fans. The first thing you need to know is that a percentage of games is rigged, so toss them out. The ones that aren't have a point spread, which basically tells the black mind that the final score is going to be in this range. At the end of the pregame shows, analysts pick the score. They are really telling you where they want your magic to make the score, and the scores they predict are always close to the spread. Do you really think some white man behind the scenes called bookies know more than professionals? They are using your magic to dictate the outcomes of games. The analysts' job is to direct you on how the game is to be played out. Let's use basketball as an example. Let's say your favorite team is down by ten points. Then your team scores two points, so they're down by eight. The next thing you know, the announcer says, "Looks like they're on a run!" How could the announcer say that after the team scored only two points? That makes no sense, but it makes more sense when you are controlling the magic. He just told black minds to make your team come back; your minds come together as one, and a miracle happens. Now the analysts' job and scouts' job is to tell you who to make the next stars. You create the stars with your magic. Your magic puts them in another realm, so that's why they stand out. They look like they're playing in the same place, but they're not. They're playing in the reality you place them in. You placed them there as being the best, like you were told, and that's why they stand out. That's why they're so against high school basketball stars going pro. It

has nothing to do with them being too young or their abilities; it has to do with them not having you create the stars. Now, they claim they have been spending more money on scouting younger talent. They're just telling you that once they change the rules, they will be able to dictate who the stars are. That's how it works. They also tell you when to kill a star's ability. This year, they told you to kill LeBron as the best player in the world, so blacks are going to fulfill that wish. Everyone understands black magic and uses black magic for their financial gains—except black people. That brings me back to the conscious community. Your consciousness is for you to protect yourself, create your own reality, and secure yourself financially, not others using your magic for themselves. Do you think the gods are stupid? You don't think we know who is asleep and who is woke? What do you think happens to the broke resistance?

ANDREW: They die.

IT: In this newly created language, the only words that are valid are *balance* and *harmony*. Throw the rest of them away. Pay attention to your enemies. They kill in the name of peace, freedom, and justice, and they tell you it's the American way.

ANDREW: Next question. Is evolution valid?

IT: No, it's made up. Blacks didn't come from apes. A dog today will be a dog tomorrow, and an elephant today will be an elephant tomorrow. Name one animal that has evolved. Your mind tells you it's wrong because it's wrong. If it doesn't make sense, it's a lie. The white man rules the planet, so he controls the knowledge. That doesn't mean you have to believe it. You have your own mind, so come up with your own truth. You don't need him to validate your truth.

ANDREW: Next question. Is the economy real?

IT: No. The economy is fake. Shown revenue is a government scam. A few big cities have real economies, but overall, no. Economy doesn't exist! Most companies are losing money like crazy. Dammit, pay attention to what you see!

ANDREW: Next question. Why is the government afraid of black people?

IT: Imagine giving an insane person access to the nuclear button. Wouldn't you be afraid of what he might do? That's the same thing with black people. They have the power to destroy the planet, and they're half asleep. That's what the fear stems from. You can take them out at any minute and they know it. Do you ever pay attention to how swiftly they remove a high-profile person when an uprising of blacks say that person is

racist and has to go? Why do you think they remove the person so quickly? It has nothing to do with morals or how you feel. It's about keeping the black mind calm. They will do backflips to get you back to sleep.

ANDREW: Another question for you, It. The big guy who claimed he lost weight from eating subs is now in jail. The crimes he was charged with are too similar to what the government charges antigovernment people with when they want to get rid of them. That's why he grabbed my attention. What's going on?

IT: Andrew, I'll answer this once we're done. Probably when I am done, you won't need the answer because you will figure it out. What is the guy famous for?

ANDREW: He's famous for making sub sandwiches popular.

IT: No, Andrew, he is famous for making cold-cut meats popular. He is also famous for making that food technology famous, and with the garnishments added, it gives the product the illusion of being healthy. He basically deceived the public. Have you ever eaten at a sub shop?

ANDREW: Yes, I have.

IT: What did you get?

ANDREW: I got the lunch combination.

IT: What does that combination consist of?

ANDREW: A sandwich, a soda, and potato chips.

IT: What combination is offered at a burger joint?

ANDREW: A sandwich, a soda, and fries.

IT: So the two are basically similar?

ANDREW: Yes.

IT: Is that a coincidence or an agenda?

ANDREW: I never paid attention to it, but now I'm curious to hear your answer.

IT: What's the lowest price you can buy a burger for?

ANDREW: About one dollar.

IT: What's the lowest price you can buy a combination for?

ANDREW: About five dollars.

IT: If you were to buy ingredients to make your own burgers, how much would it cost?

ANDREW: About twenty dollars.

IT: How many burgers could that make for you?

ANDREW: About three.

IT: So, you can only make three but buy twenty for the same price.

ANDREW: Yes.

IT: Does that make sense?

ANDREW: Not at all.

IT: Almost every product in the restaurants is imported. How are they able to sell it for less than market value and still make profit?

ANDREW: I don't know.

IT: Andrew, agendas are not for profit. They are to fulfill what they are trying to do to people. If it cost twenty dollars plus labor and travel to make three burgers, which one makes more economical sense?

ANDREW: The twenty burgers.

IT: That's how they have used economies to take away your parenting. It's easier for them to feed your kids whatever they want than you doing it yourself. When you eat at a fast food restaurant, the food you choose is not your choice; you have to choose what they present to you, and if you choose a salad, it's even worse. Most of the salad dressings have soy in them, and that's one of the most evil inventions. They portray that technology as being healthy, but people have awakened to their harmful effects. In poor neighborhoods when the women have babies, the nurses encourage them to feed their babies soy milk instead of breastmilk because it's "healthier" and "better." Common sense should tell you that what's produced naturally is always better for you than anything man-made, but those are the people you're supposed to trust. The technology of soy is rearranging kids' brains by turning Y into X and X into Y.

ANDREW: *Wow!* All across the country, why do all companies have the same combination? Do all companies think alike, or are their goals the same? It's starting to look like the same goal.

IT: How much does a twenty-ounce bottle of water cost?

ANDREW: About a dollar and fifty cents.

IT: How much does a two-liter bottle of soda cost?

ANDREW: About ninety-nine cents.

IT: Okay, Andrew, a soda has about eleven ingredients, and some of them are technology-based. Water falls from the sky; how can something free cost more than technology? It doesn't make sense. You know soda also has water?

ANDREW: Yes.

IT: It's not logical at all that it cost more. Let's move on. With all the chemicals that are in the burgers and subs and all the chemicals they spray on the garnishments when they're being grown, as soon as you eat it, your

body fights it. The most important ingredient in fries or potato chips is salt. Salt dehydrates you. Soda does two things: it dehydrates you, and when it touches your stomach, the chemical reaction makes you brave. The burp tricks you into thinking the food is digested, so after lunch your body starts fighting something invasive in the stomach, and the body begins to dehydrate because of the salt. One of the main functions of the brain is to send the chemicals your stomach needs to break down what's inside. As your body dehydrates, it takes water from the brain. With that much stress on the brain, how can it perform? Now your brain is trying to resolve what it needs to do about what's inside your stomach and prevent itself from dying at the same time. Now, with all those events happening inside your body, you begin feeling tired after lunch, so they have invented energy drinks to help speed up your dehydration process. The lunch combination is science—science that is designed to attack your brain. This is not an attack designed for blacks only; it's an attack on all people. You can't focus only on black injustice. If your view is shallow, you can easily be discredited. If you see the whole picture, your stance becomes more credible. Before I end this topic, have you ever watched people pour fries into the oil at a restaurant? How many large orders of fries can they get from one bag?

ANDREW: Maybe two.

IT: So they are losing money on the fries also?

ANDREW: Yes.

IT: This is not about money.

ANDREW: Next question. You said the Illuminati already runs the world. So why do they put out the stories about them trying to rule the world if they already do?

IT: The first thing is narrative. It's controlling your thoughts. It's the same thing as a rich person; he won't waste his time telling you he's rich. It's a waste of his time, so why would I waste my time and tell you I rule the world? My question for you is, who is your current president?

ANDREW: Donald Trump.

IT: Whom did he defeat to become president?

ANDREW: Hillary Clinton.

IT: Did the people choose the candidates, or were they given?

ANDREW: They were given.

IT: Is that freedom of choice?

ANDREW: No, it isn't.

IT: The people's job isn't to know what you think. It's all a game. It's basically choosing how you want to die. You have no freedom. That's a myth. They control the air you breathe, the water you drink, shipping, oil, airplanes, finance, and the media; you name it, and they control it. They control all presidents in every country. Blacks and whites are just as dumb. It's been in your face since the end of World War II, and you still haven't noticed it. I'll say it again—when they tell you they are trying to do something, that means they have already done it. All those so-called watchdog groups who claim they are working for the people are working for the government. Those are the people they are really working for, and those are the people who pay them. Their job is to keep your eyes closed, and their job is to keep you from seeking the truth for yourself because they are doing it for you. It's like seeing someone perform a trick. Then when you find out how the trick is done when you see it again, you're still amazed by it. They've been doing the same thing over and over, and they've been getting away with the old tricks over and over. It's to the point where they don't even try to hide it anymore. They put it in your face, and you don't see it because people see with their ears and not with their eyes.

ANDREW: Next question. Were the Egyptians the first ones on the planet?

IT: No. Blacks were here before Egyptians.

ANDREW: Next question. If the earth is millions of years old, why is it only 2019?

IT: It's only 2019 because the white man is letting you know how long he has been your god. That's what that's about.

ANDREW: Next question. In the black population, I think only about 3 percent are conscious. Am I correct with that assumption?

IT: No. You are incorrect. It's closer to 35 percent. It's just that most are underground for the same reason you don't like listening to others. Their reasons are similar. Everyone is given the same information by us, and you don't want to hear things that were already revealed. That's why they don't make themselves known.

ANDREW: Next question. If nothing is real and the leaders know it isn't real, why are they fighting so hard to keep something that doesn't exist?

IT: You all accept it as being real, so if I am in total control and if I am the god in this reality, why would I voluntarily give it up? You have to be logical. I will do whatever I can to keep it going. It's hell for you but it's heaven for them, so why would they want to leave heaven?

ANDREW: Next question. With all these people still asleep, can we still defeat our enemies if the massive awakening doesn't happen?

IT: Yes. Many different scenarios have been put in place to ensure victory. I mentioned the meditation, so here's another. Just have children. The same thing is explained with the lemonade effect; you mix the weak with the weak, and it becomes weaker. If you mix black with black, it becomes stronger. It's basically a reverse engineering process that's already taken place. Eventually you will get back to your original form. They ran the test in Germany. It was disguised as the breeding of the Über-ox. I won't be getting into details, but you can research it. The intent was to see what happens when whites breed with blacks, and the result is that, over time, you will go back to your original form as a super race. What they usually say they're doing is not what they're doing. All their studies are based on the black mysteries. Just keep that in mind when you see things.

ANDREW: Next question. Why don't we have any black holidays? After what you discussed about the *I Have a Dream* guy, I now understand that that's a white holiday given by the white man.

IT: Create your own. Stop waiting on white people to give you everything. You conscious people are missing the true point and power of the information being revealed. It's for empowerment. You have the power with your phone to access billions of people. Use what you have to create what you want. Create a Marcus Garvey Day, and have everyone take off Martin Luther King Jr. Day. Or create an "I'm not going to support white business" month. You have the power, but consciousness is just another feel-good religion. Most people only want to hear "Blacks were the original people," "The Egyptians were black," and that the Bible was stolen from Kemet. Mix that in with comedy, and another feel-good religion is born. You can't criticize the white man asking for his destruction and then turn around and have him on his hands and knees to give you something. Wake up. Create one you want. The white man worships money. If you cripple his religious person, he will make concessions.

ANDREW: Name something the white man has done that had a negative effect on his own agenda.

IT: The Internet. That's the worst thing he has created. It was created to get his message across, but it had the opposite effect. Sometimes they do things and forget the black minds are still asleep. And because the black minds are still asleep, it's easily distracted, so by not paying attention to them, they're physically killing him. They are attention vampires. Without

your attention to lend him your magic, they begin to die. Victory is not as far-fetched as you all believe. It's already in sight, but you refuse to see it. You are not putting the puzzle together correctly.

ANDREW: Next question. What is the agenda of mass shootings?

IT: It's for gun control. It's the same concept as the United Nations and the US sanctions. Take the guns away so that when they attack, there will be little resistance. That's all that's about. There are no great armies. They are all cowards who love killing people without weapons. That's how they are trained.

ANDREW: Next question. Why is it so important to get rid of the word *nigger*?

IT: It's the magic the word brings forth. That word creates anger, and anger creates destructive magic that can kill them all instantly. That goes back to the O. J. trial; that was a test run. The real purpose is black magic science. Their conclusion was that that word can kill us, so they needed to get rid of it. Use common sense. If they want to get rid of something, it's because it works in your favor. Once you hear the word *nigger* used, you don't care about any evidence. You want that person dead, and all the minds come together as one. What they're really trying to prevent is the minds coming together and causing a solar flare. That's part of the power you possess, and that's why there are so many underground facilities. They know you have the power to cause a solar flare strong enough to wipe out everything at ground level. When you hear a scientist say the sun is unstable, that's the code word for "Black people are unstable, and we need to do whatever it takes to calm them down." Everything they study is about real science, but it's really black science. When the armed forces have "black projects," they mean *black* projects. Everything is about black people. Why do you think the media and some celebrities are promoting interracial couples? It's the magic.

ANDREW: Next question. Who has mastered a portion of our magic?

IT: Phil Ivey.

ANDREW: Let's go back to mass shootings. Let's say a shooting at a popular black spot happened. What are you thinking is the answer?

IT: Now, some are real, but the real ones are usually solved. You're referring to the ones that are not solved. Most of the time familiar people attend the same venue over and over. Usually when there's a shooting and there are no suspects, it's because the patrons have never seen that person before. That person was sent there to get that establishment shut down.

Sometimes it's the government, and sometimes it's a business ritual, but it usually involves conspiracy.

Andrew: Next question. How should our lectures be priced?

It: They should be priced as high as you can possibly charge. Pay attention to our enemy's tactics. If he doesn't want you involved, he prices you out. You all need to do the same. This information is not to save your people. I already went over that. This information is for responsible people, not the everyday guy off the street or passersby. In some lectures, you all give magic spells. That's a no-no. That's giving a loaded shotgun to a child with no safety; that's disaster. Also, this information doesn't have to be validated by the people attending the lecture. The government, who also has attendees at every lecture, has a $1 trillion budget dedicated to researching everything you speak about. Do you know that if you charged $100,000 per lecture, the government would pay to attend it? So why let them in cheap? Let them pay for the information that they are going to research.

Andrew: I don't know where this "Save our people" comes from, but it's not us.

It: My next question is for you, Andrew. How old is the white race?

Andrew: A few thousands of years old.

It: How old is the black race?

Andrew: Maybe over one million years old.

It: Here is another reason you haven't been wiped out yet. If I am only two thousand years old, that's as far as my memory goes. You can only go back to your time of origin. That's how it works. You've been over one million years old, so that's how far you can go back. Your memories go back to creation and the creator. Your mind and the study of your mind is the most valuable thing on this planet. The only way to go back to the beginning is through your mind. You are the history, and you are the keeper of true history. That's why you have not been eliminated. That's at least one of the reasons. We will get into more later.

Andrew: Next question. How does a bumblebee fly with those little wings?

It: I know what you're trying to say. You can't base your conclusion on what the white man tells you. He states that the reason the bumblebee can fly with those wings that are too small for its body is because it doesn't know. Who told you that its wings are used for flight? Did it ever cross your mind that its wings are used only for control? It uses its mind for flight.

You tend to think animals and insects are stupid, but they are not. They possess intelligence. A theory is not a fact. When accepted by the majority, it's viewed as fact, but it's still just an accepted theory because people are too lazy to go beyond initial research.

Andrew: Next question. If the economy is fake and the Jews own the money, why don't they call in the money?

It: They can't. Once you make a deal with the devil, you have to be with the devil. The devil knows your secret, so you have to be loyal and play the game with him to the end. The Jews also don't want to get killed. Hitler is what keeps them in line. Also, if the white man started killing the Jews today, who would be the Jews' allies? They're hated around the world just like the blacks, so they know that they would be one of the easiest races to be wiped out. That's why they have to fall in line. I have a question for you, Andrew. Can you name a Jewish cartoon character?

Andrew: Mr. Krabs.

It: Has there ever been one episode that stated he's a Jew?

Andrew: No, it's the "money money" attitude regardless of how critical the circumstance is. No matter the danger, he only cares about money.

It: That's what I'm getting at. That's the world's view, and that's why they are hated. My next question is again yours, Andrew. How much does Queen Elizabeth make in interest each day?

Andrew: They say around $300 million.

It: Who has researched this and came up with that answer?

Andrew: The white man.

It: Has anyone in the conscious group ever disputed this claim, or is it just accepted?

Andrew: It's accepted.

It: Now, I need you to do some quick math. What's $300 million multiplied by seven days?

Andrew: A lot.

It: Can any bank pay that much interest in one week?

Andrew: Now that I think about it, no.

It: She could single-handedly bankrupt the world. Now, she is not the richest person in the world. What about Bill Gates, and what about the people from whom oil companies are leasing the pipelines? The banks pay interest also. Is that sustainable? You can't see this economy is a fraud? It's a game being played on the people. One plus one equals two. Do your own research, and do your own math. Stop using people's conclusions in your

seminars. Let them spend their trillions to research your findings, not you validating theirs. Andrew, what are government subsides?

ANDREW: They are government grants to help businesses such as farms and auto makers.

IT: What year did the civil rights movement end?

ANDREW: About 1968.

IT: What act did President Johnson pass in 1968?

ANDREW: The Civil Rights Act.

IT: Do you know the name of Title VIII of the Civil Rights Act of 1968?

ANDREW: The Fair Housing Act.

IT: This was before you were born, so let me explain this to you. While the blacks were getting duped by the march, bills were being passed under your noses to destroy you all, and everyone missed it. If you accept a check from the government, you become a government employee, and you have to follow their rules or the money will stop. I liked when you mentioned farmers because they get checks, so they have to follow the government's orders. Whatever their requirements are for you to keep receiving that check, you have to follow. In 1964 when everyone was marching and singing, "We shall overcome," President Johnson requested Congress to pass legislation to make food stamps illegal—food stamps, Section 8, and government assistance. Guess what, Andrew? Everyone who receives it becomes a government employee who has to comply with whatever the government says or else the money will stop. With the housing vouchers, government employees can live next to you and you won't even know it. So when an uprising starts, guess what. All the government has to do is arm the people on assistance and tell them that they need to kill the troublemakers or the money will stop. What do you think those people will do?

ANDREW: They probably will kill.

IT: When it comes to self-preservation, your friend becomes your foe. You think that lady or her husband on assistance will choose you over their provider? Not going to happen. Emotions are the weapon used to blind you while they are making their next chess move. They are always ahead, and everyone is so behind. It's so dysfunctional that they have groups still calling for marches. Next question, Andrew.

ANDREW: Can the world be destroyed?

IT: Yes, it can, but give me a scenario.

ANDREW: Suppose all the allies carried out a coordinated attack with nuclear weapons all over the world and dropped them at the exact same time. Would this end the world?

IT: No. That would not end the world. The only ones who would be destroyed are the soulless people. People with souls cannot be destroyed. You would wake up to another reality on earth. Now, do you see that this question makes no sense? If I make $300 million per day, why would I want my customers killed? The elites are still alive because of the people. You really think they want the people killed? They know how evil and destructive they are. Do you really think they would trust each other? If they were the only ones left, what do you think would happen? You think they would peacefully pick a ruler, or would unrest rule? They would kill each other. So that's the importance of the people and the role they play in keeping this structure together. Keep this in mind also; you can't be rich unless you have the poor.

ANDREW: Next question. Gossip—why do we view it as fact and get so upright about it?

IT: Stupidity. It's the reaction of the sleeping minds. How do you think the gods feel when you have millions of black people calling for deaths of all whites because someone said something behind their backs? I'm saying this in response to the characters depicted in movies, news, literature, and so on, but it would only be valid if it was accepted as being valid. Leave the gossip alone. Why do or should you care about what white people think? They are depicting and describing something that existed before them and before language. How can they validate you? You all need to validate yourselves. Stop attaching emotions to words, and stop asking the gods to get involved in gossip.

ANDREW: Next question. Let's go back to the end-of-the-world scenario. Can the white man still exist in the new reality?

IT: It depends on whether there is any residue left over in people's consciousness. If there is, then they will be created again, and the same story will begin again. This reality will not end without a conclusion because blacks won't let it. Until the ego is satisfied, this will have to play to the end.

ANDREW: Next question. What's the endgame of all these nuclear weapons the powers are accumulating along with other destructive technologies?

IT: It's for them to take on the gods. That's their endgame. They

want to be the rulers of the universe. They are gods of the earth, but they see beyond that. Their nature is to rule the universe. It's like the student wanting to defeat the master.

ANDREW: Is that a reachable goal?

IT: No, but that's not a subject you should waste any time or energy on. Live happily. Live in your own created reality. That's where your focus should lie.

ANDREW: Next question. You mentioned that we are eating technology. That means fake food. Why hasn't it killed us yet?

IT: It's black magic. If blacks think they are eating chicken, their magic turns it into chicken. You don't think they have wondered the same thing? Everything they try now against you fails. Now, the failure is good for research and technology advancement. They themselves suffer the majority of the casualties trying to destroy you. You've been fed paint thinner, poison, and plastic disguised as food, and you are still here. They are trying, but they can't understand the black biology and why it's so hard to destroy.

ANDREW: Next question. How outdated is the information they give us?

IT: At least forty years. When they tell you something is coming, like created food and advanced technology, you are being told what they have been doing for the last forty years. It's bull. They do it for forty years before they mention it to you. They only mention the ones that are successful. The ones that kill are the ones they never talk about. That's how it works. You really think lives matter? Andrew, I'm going to mention a few things. Some I've mentioned before that were relevant to previous topics, but everything needs to be tied together because they all serve the same purpose. Low frequency waves, high frequency waves, fluoride, fluorine, chlorine, chem trails, cigarettes, milk, soy, hot dogs, GMOs, animal antibiotics, and vaccines are all cancer cocktails. No matter how careful you are, you will be exposed to a multitude of these items each day. You don't drink pipe water, but you shower and brush your teeth with it. Guess what?

ANDREW: What?

IT: Your body absorbs it. Each day your body is being bombarded with high frequency and low frequency waves from your devices and cell towers. No one removes the batteries from their devices, so you are being hit at night when you sleep because your devices are within an arm's distance from you. Some companies have made it impossible for you to remove the batteries yourselves. Guess why?

ANDREW: Why?

IT: The big-name farmers make you buy their products to try to avoid the GMOs and antibiotics. Guess what? They're really soy factories. Have you ever wondered why soy is such a magical product? It's compatible with almost every food product. It's now more prolific than sugar and salt. View the ingredients in fresh bakeries. Walk down the aisles and pick up random food products, and soy will stick out like a sore thumb. This is now the most talked-about food product in the world. Cancer is occurring at an epidemic rate in a lot of countries, but you all don't have access to real news. You have access to the spread of fear. You even fear people thousands of miles away who will never have access to you to do any harm. Fifteen cents a day doesn't stretch far. If you have a chance to talk to people who have just arrived to America, ask them about the state of their countries. The real news will be shocking and depressing. You all really don't understand evil. You might ask, "With all this technology, why choose cancer as their weapon of choice?" And the answer is suffering and profit. Suffering for occult purposes to feed their gods and the hundreds of trillions of dollars they make off treatments that will not work; they only prolong the agony. While you're checked out, you reimburse them for living.

ANDREW: Next question. Let's go back to the Egyptian pyramids. You stated that the hieroglyphics have not accurately been decoded yet. Why is that?

IT: Some things you can solve for yourself. According to the English language, a picture is worth a thousand words. So if that's the case, have you seen any book about the pyramids that's over a million pages long?

ANDREW: No, I haven't.

IT: You can do simple math to uncover their lies. They are waiting for the black ancient minds to surface so they can fill in the blanks. Also, all things cannot be translated into language. When you present a theory challenging them, they will spend millions to discredit you publicly, then privately they'll spend trillions researching your theory because they know it's coming from an ancient mind. That's how it works. The population goes by what they see or hear publicly. That's the brainwash effect.

ANDREW: Next question. Why are we chosen for consciousness?

IT: You all are guardians of the ancient knowledge and the guardians of the sleeping ones. That's why you all were chosen. You were born with a certain compassion that makes this bigger than yourselves. You all want to do this for your people, not financial gain.

ANDREW: Next question. What's the biggest reason for reincarnation?

IT: It's the magic spell blacks made to defeat the enemy, and you will keep coming back until the wish comes to fruition. That wish is what's ruling the Earth, and all children born fall under that wish.

ANDREW: Can that wish be broken?

IT: Yes, absolutely!

ANDREW: How?

IT: We will touch on that before we end.

ANDREW: Next question. Can this information fall into the wrong hands?

IT: There's no such thing. That's universal law. There are no good hands or bad hands. This information is for everyone, even the people you deem as bad. Just view it as the truth that will set you free.

ANDREW: That's very accurate.

IT: The truth empowers you and weakens your enemies.

ANDREW: Next question. What's your biggest disappointment with the conscious community?

IT: The biggest disappointment is that with all the information given, you all haven't grouped together through meditation to break the magic spell that governs the earth. The spell you all created collectively to defeat the white man is an incomplete spell with no end. No one has taken the time to think it through.

ANDREW: What happens once the white man is defeated? Will we live happily ever after?

IT: Once they are defeated, more problems will arise. The Jews, Russians, Muslims, Africans, and Spanish will still hate you. You'll defeat one enemy, but many others will still linger. Remember, the wish is not for a reset of mind, so the same mind-set will still be in place; there will be no "happily ever after." You have to come together as one and make it right through meditation. This has to be thought through correctly for it to end. If not, this cycle will never end.

ANDREW: Once the whites are gone, who will operate the government? Who will operate transportation, trade, finance, and utilities?

IT: Who runs those systems? What about defense? You will still have enemies because the mind-set will still be exactly the same. The only change will be more wishes. You'll wish for the next enemy's destruction because no one has brought it to anyone's attention that the wish is incorrect.

ANDREW: Next question. If we come together and solve the puzzle as a unit, what will happen?

IT: A new reality begins. Many have solved it and are in a different place. They're in a place where only peace exists. You are the new laggers, the ones who are keeping this negativity together and who give your enemies life—everlasting life. When you hear people say there are many worlds and universes, has it ever occurred to you that those are the ones who solved the riddle? Open your mind. Everything is real.

ANDREW: Next question. Would you label the people on government assistance as lazy? What's your view on them?

IT: Well, Andrew, you have to always keep slavery in your mind. There were three types of slaves: the house slaves, the field slaves, and the runaway slaves. This is how it plays out in modern times: the house slaves are the people you refer to as coons, the field slaves are the hard-working blacks, and the Section 8 people are the runaway slaves. You can trace the three groups and determine who their descendants were. The wish of the runaway slaves was to never work for the white man again. The wish was granted. Now, blacks always make the statement that the white man never forgets. Who's the most brutalized by the police?

ANDREW: Low-income people.

IT: There you go. He's still punishing the slaves for running away. This is documented research that you know nothing about, but they have it. Next question is for you, Andrew. What's the most difficult thing with this conversation?

ANDREW: The most difficult task is trying to articulate it correctly. I now understand that you are 100 percent correct that the hieroglyphics have not been accurately decoded. I'm trying to document it as we go as accurately as possible, but some things cannot be translated. My words are similar, but similarity changes the meaning of the conversation.

IT: Yes, it's close but still not 100 percent accurate.

ANDREW: It's also a big eye opener for me. I now have to rethink everything I've been taught and think I know.

IT: Okay, Andrew, what's your next question?

ANDREW: The Middle East's unrest—what is it truly about? I know it's not about oil because no matter how many wars are in the region, the oil is still getting where it needs to go.

IT: There are multiple reasons. The first thing I'll touch on is money. No one can pay the cost of the oil. It's the same thing about the queen's

wealth; it's impossible to even pay the interest without killing the world's economy for the royal family. Every time Iran asks for their money, America pays them back a fraction of it. It can't be paid, and it will never be paid. It's basically hush money. The Iranians know they can't make a fuss about it because they will be bombed also. The next question is for you, Andrew. Who all was involved in slavery?

ANDREW: Whites, Hispanics, and Arabs.

IT: Where do the most persecuted women on the earth live?

ANDREW: The Middle East.

IT: That's how magic works. You have the magic of the women and the magic of the blacks at work. You just need to open your mind and pay attention. The third thing is, who are the allies of the United States?

ANDREW: The white nations.

IT: Correct. White nations were also involved in the slave trade. They are also fighting in the Middle East for the black Africans to break the magical spell placed on the white nations. They want the Africans to view them as liberators and release the spell. You all truly don't understand black magic or its true power. The white powers think steps ahead. When you think they are doing one thing, they are doing that one thing to accomplish multiple things. Number one on that list is how to break the spells placed on them.

ANDREW: Next question. Are there really four seasons on earth?

IT: No. There is only one, and it's winter. The other three are controlled by the black minds. That's why blacks were placed on the planet—to give it life. If you didn't exist, earth would be a frozen ice ball. When the weaker man says it's spring, what do black people say?

ANDREW: We say it's not going to be cold anymore.

IT: And what happens?

ANDREW: It starts to warm up.

IT: There you go. Your minds work together and change the weather. That's how your magic works. In summer, you all say it's going to get hot, and the wish gets granted. In fall, you say the trees are going to start changing, and in winter you say it's going to be cold. That's how it works. That's also how the white man manipulates you all to work your magic for them. So imagine once you all figure it out and use your magic for yourselves.

ANDREW: What happens when we figure it out and use our magic against them?

IT: That's their greatest fear. That's the fear that helps keep you all alive. It's not the only reason you're alive, but it's one of them.

ANDREW: Next question. Why did the elites take over the music industry?

IT: Bob Marley. They will not allow that kind of magic to happen again. He brought too many minds together to work as one. That's also what got him eliminated in the little view, but overall, his job was done. Blacks fall for the same trick over and over. The whites—well, it only happens once, and then they set practices to make sure it never happens again. These are the things you have to set in place if you want to rule forever.

ANDREW: Next question. Are whites smarter than blacks?

IT: No. Smarter doesn't exist. Blacks have an ancient mind, as we've discussed before. Whites created the language. Blacks are the most studied, and everything you see now came from the black mind. Also, the depiction of the white man as always being the hero is the same script whites have been shown, so they are just as brainwashed as blacks. The government would never just do that. That's not stupidity; that's coming from a genuine place. They honestly don't know. They're most affected by the brainwash because it's been done by people they perceive to be their own.

ANDREW: Next question. There's ancient scripture documenting that blacks were going to be enslaved. Why?

IT: Everything that happens has to happen. See, everyone thinks the blacks who sold the slaves were stupid. Never think that way. They also understood the ancient scripture and sold who was supposed to be sold. Do you remember the Mariel boatlift?

ANDREW: Yes. That's when Castro sent all the criminals to America.

IT: So do you ever think about why those blacks were sent to America? Do you think the whites were happy with the product they received? The white man ended up with a thorn in his side that he can't get rid of. The resistance was sent out. Anytime someone willfully gives you something, it's usually not for your benefit, and slavery is a perfect example. It's a black eye they can never get rid of, and it's a black eye that other nations throw in their face when they try to act righteous. This is the way this evil needed to be exposed. Open your mind more, view the bigger picture, and think about strategy. Time doesn't exist, so what you think is hundreds of years of persecution is only a fraction of time. You guys speak before you analyze. Emotions cloud reality.

ANDREW: Next question. Why did the American colonists fight the British?

IT: First of all, it was the British fighting the British. The Americans were British; they just stole the natives' land and called it their own.

ANDREW: Also, aren't the British and the Americans allies?

IT: Yes, so why would your enemy be your ally? It's all a big game. America is still under British rule. That was just another part of the puzzle in order to obtain world domination, which they now have.

ANDREW: Next question. What dominates day-to-day reality?

IT: Money. They stage events to become more wealthy. No matter what event, disaster, or whatever, the money always seems to end up in the hands of the elites. You can make a great living by just tracing where all the money ends up. There is no coincidence. That doesn't exist anymore. Things are also staged to be viewed as biblical prophesies. You can't end the lies. They have to continue to justify this reality.

ANDREW: Next question. I heard two stories: one was about a woman in ancient times, and the other was about Buddha. I don't want to get into details because it has no relevance. What *is* relevant is that these were the first times I heard these stories and something basically—how can I put this?—replay the events in my head. Can you explain this?

It replays the events in Andrew's head.

IT: Maybe the stories were actually you in a previous life. That's why you had flashbacks. That's also why a first story is so vivid. I drew an ancient memory of yourself, or you were around and witnessed those events as they transpired.

ANDREW: Next question. How many people am I?

IT: You are more than one individual. Since creation, just add two to this current day. That's your makeup. All that's a part of your DNA, and you have access to all of that information. That's why your mind is so valuable. All the knowledge, trials, and tribulations—you have access to everything each one of your bloodline went through. You are also blessed with any powers they had.

ANDREW: Next question. Why did the Egyptians mummify themselves?

IT: What does a caterpillar do before it turns into a butterfly?

ANDREW: It wraps itself into a cocoon.

IT: What's the purpose?

ANDREW: To protect its body during the transformation process.

IT: There's your answer. You can't go with the white man's interpretation

of something that took place before language. It's also a message left for you all that blacks are in the morphing stage. The white man knows this. He took an egg from Africa that's starting to morph into a dragon. The people they brought from Africa are their destruction. That's what dragon movies are about—the black metamorphosis. You have to be able to see and understand the bigger picture. That's what consciousness is about. Once you understand it, you need to articulate it as understandably for all as possible. That's how you can help many transition into the next phase.

ANDREW: Next question. As we are currently speaking, where are we actually?

IT: We are currently in the realm of information. You are in my reality. In your time, you have been here for seven days so far. You haven't slept, eaten, used the bathroom, or gotten tired. Information is the food that has sustained you for the past seven days. Everyone's current life is based on what they have been told and taught. Language has rendered hundreds of you all useless. Some people are not smart enough to know their own damn powers because the white man has already done research for you, and no one takes the time to go further because you are afraid to challenge him, and disprove his theories. Andrew, have you ever seen some of the amazing things autistic children can do?

ANDREW: Yes, things science can't explain currently.

IT: Do you think they were born with that defect, or were they sent down?

ANDREW: I don't know. I've never really thought about it that way.

IT: Their lack of comprehension is why it's so easy for them to tap into their powers. Imagine how destructive it would be. Start understanding what you see and not what you're told to understand. If you can imagine it, it's because it's inside you, and you just have to unlock it. Now, some autistic children are that way because of vaccines. That's done on purpose, so we alter a few to send a message to the mass. You just have to decode it. It's also a way to make them rethink the vaccines. More and more powerful autistic children will come forth—the real superhumans. Pay close attention, and don't let it slip by you.

ANDREW: Next question. The new trend now is to save the planet by using less water and fossil fuels. What's your take on that?

IT: Do you pay attention to chem trails? What about fluorine and fluoride in the drinking water, and what about pesticides? Does your government even act like it cares about the planet?

ANDREW: No … it doesn't.

IT: So why would you listen to a trend they started? Your job is to live as balanced as possible. Try to live as one with nature the best way you can with the obstacles that are placed in front of you. Don't be so quick to jump on any trend. When they show that they care, then you follow. What's the game when people do something positive and then turn around and do what they tell you not to do? It makes no sense at all. Trends are usually a money grab. Once the trend loses steam, they come up with another one.

ANDREW: Next question. Why are Asian people so smart?

IT: It's because of the written language. It's an ancient language that uses symbols, and because it is so complex, the brain has to work much harder than it does when using the English language. The harder the task is that the brain has to do, the smarter you become. Now, I'm just using the word *smarter* to explain this the best way I can. Truly, smarter doesn't exist. What exists is the ability to tap into certain realms just like you tapped into the information realm. There is a technology realm, a sports realm, a music realm, and the list goes on. What you all view as smart isn't real. Individuals have the ability to tap into other realms.

ANDREW: Next question. There are a lot of people who are now going off the grid. Is that a good idea?

IT: If you understand the design of the system that's in place that you all have to live by, you will then realize that it's not a good idea at all. First of all, who is their representation in government? If the government violates their rights, who speaks on their behalf? They can charge you with tax evasion or any other crime they choose to, and no one would make a whimper about it. The media won't cover it because they work for the government. The only freedom you have is the right to participate in the system and its design. If you are so-called off grid, that means I can't profit off of you. That makes you useless. If I incarcerated you, you are back in the system and accounted for. If you want to live a little better in prison, you need to work for me for fifteen cents per day. Andrew, always have your eyes open for the bigger picture.

ANDREW: Next question. What are clouds?

IT: Clouds are consciousness. They are the souls of many of your dead ancestors who refused to be reincarnated. That's why you all are able to control the weather so easily. Also, they are the souls of millions of Native Americans and buffaloes. Did it ever occur to you that tornadoes are a result of the dead buffalo migration? Energy never dies. It keeps going.

What you do in life, some also do in death. Energy doesn't die. With the physical body, consciousness remains and conscious things are still being performed because the energy remains.

Andrew: Next question. What are wind turbines for?

It: Generating electricity. My question for you, Andrew, is, where are most of the wind turbines in the United States located?

Andrew: The north and west areas.

It: That's usually high ground, or you can call them mountain areas. Mountain areas are where you would have the most government facilities. What powers those facilities? Would you tell your enemies that wind turbines are used for that specific purpose?

Andrew: Absolutely not.

It: They are all located in the middle of nowhere just spinning with the wind. You all need to do more thinking and analyzing while observing. It's always about the bigger picture.

Andrew: What about underground transport? Where do they get their power?

It: Andrew, you have to think. The answers are right in your face. You just have to ask yourself the questions. There are no questions that you can't get the answers to. All you have to do is ask. It might not be revealed to you the same day, but eventually it will be revealed. Spirits are not limited by physical bodies. Spirits can go almost anywhere. There are some places where there is technology in place where spirits can't go. Your enemies aren't dumb. They also thought about it and researched these questions many years ago and put things in place to prevent security breaches. What you are detailing might be new to many but is old information to some.

Andrew: Next question. You mentioned some of the most powerful black minds in the United States. Why is that? You will have to add the Caribbean to that list, and you have to exclude Haiti and most African nations from that list.

It: There is a cap on those countries' educational development. It's all by design. If a little country can defeat Napoleon, you think they would want to educate them? If you were that destructive, imagine what you would be now if you had access to the information we have now—not the misinformation project that you all are getting. Real information. African nations are still being punished for the slave trade. The allies despise everyone involved with the slave trade because they don't like the product that was sold to them. They were sold their destruction, so they will have

to keep paying the price. There are other reasons, like the theft of minerals, but you have to have knowledge about all things. My first answer is more in line with your topic and people you are trying to reach and open minds.

ANDREW: My next question is about California wildfires. I know wildfires pop up all around the country, but this seems abnormal to me. Why?

IT: It seems abnormal because it is abnormal. These fires are being set. Californians wants to be separated from the United States, and they are making arrangements to be their own country, so they have to be punished. Have you ever seen a Middle Eastern country trying to launch a satellite?

ANDREW: Yes, I have.

IT: What usually happens?

ANDREW: They usually fail.

IT: Have you ever seen a launch failure on television?

ANDREW: Yes I have.

IT: Now, you are telling me that those people who are spending billions on research and technology can't launch a satellite? You have to be smarter than that, Andrew. When you're able to pull up a failed launch video, pay close attention to the point of failure. You will see it was shot down by a laser from another satellite. The white man thinks space belongs to him and his allies only. That means only white people, so when any other nation tries, they shoot them down. I can also start a wildfire with the same technology.

ANDREW: Next question. There is a big push now for our farmers to use genetically modified seeds. Should we be concerned about this?

IT: Yes, but there is nothing you can do about it. You think those people are going to spend trillions on technology to accomplish a goal and let you refuse? Because of the trillions they've invested, they have to make many trillions in profit on top of that. For any farmer who resists, their crops will be murdered, they will be forced to sell their land to someone who will go with the plan, or the government will find an endangered species on their land and take it. Finally, what happens when all their partners refuse to buy their products? There are many protocols set in place to ensure that they continue their agenda.

ANDREW: What impact will be these modified foods have on us?

IT: That's not for anyone to worry about. You have been eating bananas and other modified foods, and you just haven't been aware of it. Whatever

they do, we will send newborns who are immune to it. The more they up the ante, the stronger the people we send will be. That's how it works.

ANDREW: Next question. Why is there such a big push in all states to legalize marijuana?

IT: My question for you, Andrew, is, whose face do most people associate with marijuana?

ANDREW: Well, It, it's Bob Marley.

IT: So he is more recognized for marijuana than his liberation music?

ANDREW: That's correct.

IT: The reason there is a big push now is because the research is complete, and the genetically modified strains of marijuana are completed and ready for consumption. What people are smoking now is not the same thing Bob Marley was smoking. This is now a synthetic drug with opposite effects. The debates your government has are just a smokescreen for people. Don't pay attention to them. This is what they accomplish with the marijuana: they screw everyone up and the face of it is Bob Marley, so that's how you kill him. Now he's the face that's screwing up the new generation. They are always thinking steps ahead.

ANDREW: Next question. A lot of Native American populations are being devastated by drugs. What's the reason behind it?

IT: Have you ever heard the term *designer drugs*?

ANDREW: Yes, I have.

IT: That means it's being designed for you. All of these drugs have been studied for years before they got put on the market. The creators spend millions on research and design. Most of the public thinks that someone in a backyard shed is making the drugs because that's what the news shows the public during the raids. Someone in the shed is not a chemist. These are invented by professionals. Also, drugs are actually part of a real economy. The money never stops coming because the drugs were designed for addiction. The Native Americans who are in trouble are the resistance. They are the ones who never settled with the government about how evil they are; the government stole their land, and that's what the drugs were designed for. It was designed to silence the resistors.

ANDREW: Next question. Let's go back to slavery. Most black prisoners are from a low-income background. Are most of them descendants of runaway slaves?

IT: Yes. Now, in prison you are a recaptured slave. The runaway slaves were never granted their freedom, or they paid for their freedom. They

had a negative impact on profits. You think the enemy that never forgives and forgets will let that go? So now that you're in prison, you have two jobs. You can either work in the factory for them for twenty cents per day to help pay for the economic impact that your parents had on the cotton business when they ran away, or your other option is to pick up paper on the expressway. For those who know, picking up paper on the expressway represents picking cotton, so you are back to doing what your parents were brought here to do. If you try to escape again, the police have shoot-to-kill orders.

ANDREW: Next question. There are a lot of real white people who are waking up now. What triggered the awakening?

IT: September 11. That incident opened a lot of white people's eyes. When injustice is directed toward another race of people, it's easy to look the other way, but when it's directed at you and what the government says happened and what you saw happen don't line up, that's going to wake you up. Now, with this ground destined for the government brewing for years, they have to come up with a plan to direct the awakening to something else, so you offer them the show *Ancient Aliens* to capture their imagination of the glories of space and its potential and a place for whites. Who are the faces of everything relating to space and aliens?

ANDREW: David Wilcock and Dr. Steven Greer.

IT: You know the government. What happens to anyone who goes against the government?

ANDREW: There are either dead or in prison.

IT: So you have these two people releasing government documents with new technology, government black projects, space technology, and more, and they're still alive. Does that add up, Andrew?

ANDREW: Not at all.

IT: They kill people for anything, including singers. These people have access to informants, documents, new and old technology, and alien races, and they're still alive. This is your government at work. They offered the awakened whites something to grab onto and something to capture their attention regarding a new future that involves space and a future without blacks. It worked. They can't get enough of this space thing now. They're flooding theaters, television shows, and cartoons with this stuff and making billions in the process. The government plays poker with the people; they are always moves ahead. Unless you change the way you and

each and every one of you, meaning blacks and good whites, think, you all will always be playing catch-up.

ANDREW: Next question. Does the government even care about what the people think or say?

IT: Who is your president right now, Andrew?

ANDREW: Donald Trump.

IT: What does he do?

ANDREW: He says and does anything he wants. He operates like he is above humanity and the law.

IT: There's your answer.

ANDREW: Next question. Back to the alien theme. Where does this lead?

IT: For the last forty or fifty years, have you heard that the government is going to stage a mock alien invasion?

ANDREW: Yes. There are many books on that.

IT: So the population is forty to fifty years behind. Now, David Icke does the same kind of lectures, correct?

ANDREW: Yes.

IT: He lives in England, correct?

ANDREW: Yes.

IT: That's a US ally, correct?

ANDREW: Yes.

IT: Everyone has been conditioned for the stage you all are at now—the space exploration. Now, Andrew, what do you think the alien invasion is going to be about?

ANDREW: I can't answer that question because it's something I haven't thought about.

IT: The first thing is, an alien invasion is a great way to lead a majority of the population to join the military. Do you remember when George W. Bush said he went to reinstate the draft?

ANDREW: Yes, I do.

IT: That's because people are finding better opportunities than the military. What a smart way to unite for the planet. As evil as these people are, where would do you think they would stage the alien attacks?

ANDREW: I would think they would stage them in the United States and England.

IT: Now the allies will come together to fight the aliens. Once the aliens are contained, they will stage the new alien attacks in the Middle

East, Africa, and every predominantly black country. That's how you rid the earth of aliens. The only blacks who will remain are the ones in the military, and most of them will be under mind control. That's why in most alien movies, you will probably see one or two black people. Let's say the narrative is that one alien carries a contagious virus that can wipe out the planet. If one alien enters Africa, what will the allies do, Andrew?

ANDREW: Wipe out that continent because it becomes a matter of national security.

IT: Now you're thinking.

ANDREW: Next question. Were we put on this planet to suffer until the end?

IT: I'll answer this question regarding blacks in America—not worldwide. What you call suffering is not being able to live the same way you precieve the white race does. You want to own businesses, control commerce, and have the ability to buy some things they call luxurious. That's suffering now. However, universally, that's not suffering at all. That's ego. You have to recognize the flaw in mentality. Ego isn't suffering. When the white man used the flamethrower on you and lynched you, that was suffering, but what you call suffering now is not being able to buy the same items they're able to buy, live in the same homes as they can, and have the same jobs they have. Now if what you call suffering is breathing contaminated air, drinking poisonous water, and eating modified foods, then yes that's suffering, but everything now is based on fulfilling the ego. It's misguided. You all are basically equating the needs of ego as suffering. If you want the world changed because it's being run with a flawed design that doesn't create fair value for people, that's valid. There is too much talking and not much thinking. The thought process is off. Many conscious people sound educated, but you can point out many flaws. The biggest flaw is the ego. Until the minds come together correctly and are pure of heart, nothing will change. If you think the suffering will never end, it won't because of the flaws. "Kill all the whites because I need money" is also not valid. That only empowers your enemies in every country. When you document the inequities and unjustness, they can write it off by saying, "If you work harder, you can achieve the same." They know it's ego, and ego is easy to expose. That's why they can laugh at you and degrade you. You all keep providing ammunition for them to use against you.

ANDREW: Next question. Will the soulless white imposter win?

IT: What do you mean by *win*, Andrew?

ANDREW: Will they succeed in wiping us off the planet?

IT: That's another question that doesn't really make sense. If all blacks die, you're dead, so why would you care? Just think about that. What if death gives you the life to defeat them? Spiritually, you are much stronger than you are physically. In spiritual form, you become a god and you have your god powers. When you are asleep, you are in a spiritual state, and that's why you can fly and do whatever and go wherever you want. The ego is against death. Energy never dies. You cannot be destroyed. Only the physical can be destroyed. Has it occurred to you that the white man with no soul that you're fighting is ego? He's the real ego. That's what was extracted from you to create him. You are fighting ego with ego. You all have to solve this puzzle. No one should have to come and provide the solution. Pay attention to all the things he has been doing for over a thousand years. Evaluate it. It's 100 percent ego. The enemy is the ego, and you can't defeat ego with ego. You are more similar than different. They are your brothers, but they're the dark half and your mom's favorite. They have all the luxury in life, and you have the soul. That's what the war is about. You hate each other for what the other possesses. What you all view as consciousness is still asleep but just slightly awakened. Solve the puzzle, and then the reality will change.

ANDREW: Next question. Has the white man proven anything?

IT: Yes. He has proven to the world that if you are descendants of the gods, you all were descended from a weak and inferior god. He is going to live his existence as a powerful god because this is his reality, and that's what he has shown so far. He rules with an iron fist, and as gods, you have no reason to criticize. Your job is to worship every Sunday. He is the judge, jury, and executioner. When people suggest to blacks that they should start being gods, they are afraid of some sort of punishment, so universally you all would rather keep getting kicked in the ass. Everything you refuse to do because of some moral or whatever, they do. You want your enemy dead, but your enemies are better at being you than you are. He is the perfect imposter. He has perfected being the imposter. Andrew, remember the list of names I gave of people who made it to the god level? Add your enemies to the list. They are the ones who designed the system they live by.

ANDREW: Next question. Were there any positives from the Million Man March?

IT: Yes indeed, Andrew. Louis Farrakhan is a very intelligent man. Now, he was a double agent working for both sides. The Million Man

March basically just let the white man know that even though I'm working for you, I still have the power to destroy you. The million is a correct number for destruction. All you need is the black minds working together for a single objective to level the planet. Don't think he thought of that number out of the blue. That number was revealed to him. Sometimes the messages were revealed to him, and sometimes the message is more important than a person's character. Character is always used to discredit the message. Don't fall for that. Sometimes the most important messages come from the worst people. If you are a true seer, you only care about the message, not the deliverer of the message. Next thing, Andrew. Let's go back to 9/11. I need to elaborate a little more because you all have to understand the bigger picture. The leaders don't deal with micro. It's always about macro. September 11 was about research. It was done to see if whites would be awakened, but big-picture wise, if it had been a mass attack on blacks, they would have awakened. All scenarios are staged. The big picture is, how can the black race be wiped out without their coming online? September 11 showed them that any mass murders against blacks will have to be done in secret. This was all a test run. After every event, they get back to doing research. They never leave any stone unturned. You have to be diligent, and as rulers of the planet, they are. Next question.

ANDREW: Okay, It. Are black people chaotic beings?

IT: That's one of the questions I've been waiting on for the past nine days. That's a great analogy that ties a lot of things together. The reason most black people aren't waking up and becoming more conscious is because, where's the chaos? Chaos is what activated your melanin, and that's what activates your consciousness. If a threat of extinction ever occurs, everyone would come online at the same time to prevent it. The planet can't exist without blacks, and it's not for the reason you might think. Without you, the planet dies. It will become a huge ice ball in the sky, and eventually everyone will die. Technology might hold it up for a little while, but eventually all the life will cease to exist on earth. Andrew, I'm going to name a few things: the first is *MTV Cribs*, the second thing is college signing days, third is the NFL and NBA, and the last one is Will Smith. I would ask you what you think, but you will get it wrong so I'll just tell you. This is how conscious speakers get discredited and get viewed as lost people who don't live in this reality. Before you all can even speak, your enemy puts the evidence against everything you speak about in the public view for both whites and blacks to see. So when people say blacks are poor,

everyone saw the black superstar's mansion on MTV, so that's lie number one. When people say blacks don't have opportunity, you send your kids to college for free, so that's lie number two. When people say America is racist, they gave you a black president, so that's lie number three. When people say blacks lack opportunities, look at all of the black players in the NFL and NBA who are making millions, and some billions. Andrew, do you really know who you are fighting against? He has you defeated in the public view before you can make any claims. Whites and blacks will view you all as crazy because of what he implanted subliminally in their minds. If you all want to wake people up, you have to be better prepared. Do more research before any attack is launched. The only other option is to wait for the chaos to end.

ANDREW: Next question. With them always being steps ahead of us, is the conscious community wasting its time?

IT: You all were gifted that ability for a purpose. You have exposed pasts, conspiracies, and future plots not only against blacks but humanity as a whole. They spend trillions on research, and we help level the playing field by giving you all trillions worth of dollars of information exposing them. Imagine how they feel having to spend tens of trillions on a secret plan, and you guys expose it before it even gets off the ground. That's trillions of dollars in the garbage. Now they have to spend more money trying to figure out how it got exposed and finding a breach in their own group. It's a never-ending game, and a lot of money is being wasted on it, so they're always back to the drawing board. You all have no idea how many lives you all have saved. The impact of your effort is not wasted. It's time that's well spent, and it's a final disaster for your enemies.

ANDREW: Next question. We end up making more white people conscious than blacks. Is that a good thing?

IT: Yes, it is. In the big picture, it's great. White people have the voice in this system's design. As the white imposter, you have to cater to them so your cover isn't blown. The real white people who always protest with you are armed, and they have a distrust of the government. The Constitution is their Bible, and they have no problem defending it with their lives. There are countless steps being taken now to disarm the population, like staging events. White people will not give up their weapons. They are already preparing for the fight and the power that they know.

ANDREW: It, I have a comment for you. Some of the answers you have provided me with are not what I expected. I guess I was expecting

everything to be preconscious, but it's not. It's some on both sides, for and against.

IT: No, let me stop you right there. It's all preconsciousness. You can't have a narrow mind. You have to see the bigger picture. Some will believe it that way, but once you finally understand, then it will all make sense.

ANDREW: Next question. I need you to address Haiti a little bit more. There was an earthquake there that I believe was staged. Now we have an expresident over there playing the white hero again. When the political unrest was going on there and thousands of innocent lives were being taken, the United States refused to intervene. Why the sudden interest?

IT: The first thing is natural resources. Money is always number one on the list when the government shows interest. They will provide millions in aid and rob the country of billions in resources. That's the narrow view; the most important thing is voodoo. They want it. If that power can be obtained, they want it. Also, there are a lot of Haitians living in America. That scares them. They don't want it used against them in a civil unrest, so they're back to doing research on voodoo again. Now America is the face of what's going on, but the intel they are trying to gather is for America and its allies.

ANDREW: Next question. Did voodoo really defeat Napoleon? Something you mentioned earlier tells me no.

IT: Andrew, what's the magic in Haiti?

ANDREW: Voodoo.

IT: So when Napoleon ran out of there and they came back as tourists asking the natives how they defeated Napoleon, they said voodoo. So logically there is no way Napoleon could have been defeated, so the voodoo magic got the credit. Where is the origin of voodoo?

ANDREW: Africa.

IT: Is it still being practiced there?

ANDREW: Yes, and in many countries on other continents. The names might be different, but it's the same thing.

IT: The white man is still on the rampage in Africa, correct?

ANDREW: Yes.

IT: So, why hasn't the magic expelled him?

ANDREW: I don't know.

IT: The last magical spell to kick the white man's butt in Africa was cast by Bob Marley. It was in the form of a song called "Zimbabwe." What you think of as music is really magical spells if written correctly. It cost him

his human life, but his job was fulfilled. Back to voodoo. Andrew, does everyone in Haiti practice voodoo?

ANDREW: No, and that's the same for every country that practices that kind of magic. It's usually a small portion of the population, and they usually fire guns.

IT: Andrew, chaos happened. When the most powerful army enters a small island like Haiti for war, that brings on the threat of extinction for all the natives, so we brought everyone online. When everyone comes online, you have total control of all energies that ever existed on that island. All your dead ancestors, animals, trees, and everything else that ever lived is the power that gets unleashed. There are stories about the army turning guns on themselves, but no—the spirits were the ones shooting them in the heads. You have to stop thinking the white man is the authority on everything. He has provided theories on everything, and it's taken as facts; but it's all theories. He has no clue how things really work. He calls it supernatural, which is the code for "It's over my head." If it can't be physically analyzed, it's not real to him. His power is science and technology. Your power is the control of all energy that ever existed, and you all have the access to release that energy when the time comes. We brought Haiti online. Let them keep spending money on researching voodoo. It's powerful magic, but energy is what defeated Napoleon. Andrew, if I didn't let you know already, I'm reading your mind. There is no question you ask that I don't already know you're going to ask, and some I implanted in your mind for you to ask.

ANDREW: Next question. The United States has been in Iraq since 2003. Something about this war is not adding up. What is it?

IT: It's a trick. You all get fooled too easily, and no one asks any questions. You're telling me that the most powerful army in the world who has the nuclear capacity to level the planet is in a sixteen-year war with eighty-year-old ladies who strap bombs to eleven-year-old boys? When they show a video, it has about five people getting blown up. This is what you guys fall for? You can destroy the world with the touch of a button, but sixteen years later, there's still no resolution. Why is no one asking the question? Or is America's government misleading its people about their capabilities? Fear is one of their biggest money makers. Fear prints money. They've been fighting viciously, but the oil is still moving and the president is always shaking hands with the oil leaders. The people are never provided any real evidence that there's even a real war being fought. I don't want to get into details because it's not relevant to what we are discussing. Before I

exit, I can go into a little more detail, but this is not for public consumption. The questions I put forth are where everyone's mind needs to be, and it's not only the United States over there. Their allies are there also.

Andrew: Next question. What's the purpose of countries' invading other countries when a critical part of their mission is to destroy that country's artifacts?

It: It's to erase history. As an adult, when you pass on ancient history to your kids, you don't have to convince them of what you're saying; the artifacts are there for you to show them. With no artifacts to show them, it becomes a fictional story with no evidence to prove your teachings. If you want to own history, that has to be a major part of your mission so you can destroy what's there and insert your own. Eventually, your inserted history becomes the truth.

Andrew: Next question.

It: Before we get back, I have a comment for you.

Andrew: Go ahead, It.

It: If you're ever late for anything, never rush to get there. There is no real difference in being ten or fifteen minutes late. Why kill yourself to save two minutes so you're late eight minutes instead of ten? In order to maintain balance, there are certain unfortunate events scheduled for certain individuals. It might so happen that you and that individual might be crossing paths at the same time of the event, and we made you late to avoid that event. Your being late is a gift, not a curse. If you lose your job, that's also supposed to happen. Everything that happens is in your best interest, even if it doesn't seem so at the time. I chose the word *kill* for that reason. Even though it's not scheduled for you, you will become a casualty of that event, so just keep that in mind.

Andrew: Next question. If a mass attack begins, and we are not online, is there anything we can do to help with the battle?

It: You all should start speaking about what process needs to take place in case it does happen. This subject should be covered in all conscious meetings. The meetings need to cover death, and everyone needs to know what their duties and responsibilities are to continue the fight. Once you give the instructions, their spirits are bound. They cannot go into the light until their obligations are fulfilled. That's why they can currently get away with doing whatever they want and kill whomever they want. No one has taken the time to give instructions and assigning responsibilities that have to be fulfilled. Andrew, do you see how easy this is? I know you feel kind

of stupid now, but don't. This had to be revealed. In all the BS marches you all participated in in the past, the only positive to come from them is the understanding that your powers are greater than any physical weapons. You don't need weapons to win. All you need is instructed casualties. Death is actually life—unstoppable life. If you all get online, then you have control of all energies that have passed. When you give instructions, you have access to everyone who was instructed. You can't be narrow-minded with the instructions. It has to be big picture, and it has to be free-the-world instruction, not win-one-battle instruction. Get it?

Andrew: I really do, It.

It: Andrew, do I need to elaborate a little more on this?

Andrew: No, I get it. Next question. It might be off topic, but why do so many black children have no fathers?

It: Slavery is the answer. Before slavery, Africans only knew the family structure, such as the mother, father, and children, but with many descendants in the same home. The white man broke up the family structure. He stole the fathers and mothers from the children, or if it was a complete family that was sold, he separated them. When they arrived on the plantation in whatever country they were sent to, what did he do? He raped the woman and left the children he didn't kill fatherless. We can also tie it back to the runaway slaves he is still attacking. Some of them are his children. On a side note, do you know that Al Gore's great-grandfather was a slave master? There is great success in separating the family. It weakens it. He is still doing it today; it's called deployment. You can fill in the rest. But the magic is as strong when the family is incomplete. Also, before we get to the next question, I refer to you all as blacks, and you do also. However, you are not black. Your tone can't be translated in this language. As stated earlier, you all predate language. When you all fell to the physical, this was the form you were given. We can dive into this a little later.

Andrew: Next question. What is the purpose of the soul?

It: Just think of it as the Internet. The soul is what links you all to everything in the universe. Your soul is what gives you the ability to control everything in the universe. On earth, you control all elements and all life. It also makes you one with the gods; it gives you everlasting life. Once the ones without souls die, that's it. So that's why it's imperative for them to live as gods now because, once they die, it ends. The soul is where your superpowers are located. When you lose your physical form, you become the Superman, the invisible man, and a god, but without instructions,

you will travel. You will spend more time trying to figure out what you have become. The amazement will lead you astray. If instructed, you will unleash the power on anyone who threatens you. Earlier I told you the clouds in the sky are souls. Most people just use them to control the weather, but those souls are a part of your universal army waiting for your instructions. The soulless people cannot control souls; only people with souls can instruct other souls. Chem trails are the white man's way of trying to control those souls. Everything they do is through technology. Hell, if you want to do it, why shouldn't they? They are poisoning everything you control. Look at all these untapped powers you all have access to and are not taking advantage of. Instead of using your powers, you blame the gods. The white man studies your powers. You asked for help because you were told your powers are bad and black magic is evil, and the white god is going to punish you if you use it. You know who scares them? The so-called black people who go to the graveyard to steal souls. No, they are not stealing souls. They are bonding the souls to earth so they can't leave until their instructions are completed. What you view as some sort of power or magic is all of your natural abilities. They still practice these abilities and practice as hired sons. Let's move on.

ANDREW: Next question. I've read and heard things saying that a lot of leaders are run by artificial intelligence. I've also heard that some armies and police officers are also run by artificial intelligence. What happens if they unleash them against us?

IT: Nothing. I've already explained it to you. You all are electrical beings, so you have the ability to control anything that has electrical parts. I'll say this again: start giving the living instructions on their responsibilities when they pass. That needs to be included in all your meetings. Also, teach your family members the same. Don't waste time worrying about extermination projects. Start preparing everyone to be victorious.

ANDREW: Next question. What happens if the white man with no soul succeeds in graduating us from earth? What happens next?

IT: That's the diploma they are facing. People with souls can never die. You all just jump realities. The only ones who can die are the ones with no souls. That's the end for them. One way or another, their end will come. It might not be by your hands or their hands. There are many realities. Some are physical like the one you are currently a part of, and some are spiritual realities. You can end up somewhere better or somewhere worse. It depends on the individual. Before we get to the next question, Andrew,

you have to learn how to turn everything in life into a math equation. Once you understand how to do that, you can solve a lot of the mysteries I have revealed to you. If it doesn't make sense, turn it into a math problem, and then you can come up with the correct solution. I don't know if this is over your head, but a lot of people will understand that concept. Math is universal. It's the most consistent truth on earth. Language is the trick of the land. Egyptians were masters of mathematics, and they left everyone the blueprint on how to access universal truth.

ANDREW: Next question. The story of Jesus was taken from the Egyptian hieroglyphics about the sun. They creatively turned it into the *son*. What is the sun?

IT: The sun is what terrorizes your enemy. We discussed the solar flares earlier, and I thought you would have figured out the answer by now. Andrew, have you noticed that, all over earth, dark-skinned people have a hard time waking up early?

ANDREW: Yes. It's one of the mysteries I want solved!

IT: What happens when the sun hits dark skin?

ANDREW: We absorb it.

IT: What happens when it hits white skin?

ANDREW: It burns.

IT: The word *absorb* is a good word. If you put a dry sponge in the water, what does it do?

ANDREW: Absorbs the water.

IT: Why didn't you say it stores the water?

ANDREW: I didn't think of it that way.

IT: What if that energy is being stored and released? Blacks are the life of the planet. That's the purpose of all of you—to keep it alive. You all are the sun. There is no sun 93 million miles away. The Egyptians told you all that you're the sun, and somehow it was missed. Why do you think the Sphinx is facing east? It's marveling at your creation. It's the creation of life. If blacks die, the sun dies. That's why you all are so tired in the morning. You give off enormous amounts of energy each day and night and don't even realize it. Your physical bodies know this, and that's why they're so tired in the morning. You all are the everyday life of the planet. The four seasons do not exist. You're all tricked into creating the seasons. When you all hear *summer*, you say it's going to be hot, and it gets hot. It's the same for the other three seasons. I explained that earlier, so I won't again. That's

the mystery that they didn't want you all to over discover. You have heard them say that the earth may end by fire, correct?

ANDREW: Yes, I have.

IT: They are just letting whites know that once blacks figure it out, they will use the sun to destroy them. You see, Andrew, there is no need for the gods to intervene in your battle. You all have great gifts. Your gifts are dominant for a reason. You all are the gods of life, not the gods of destruction. Also, realize that every time you speak, you create a magic spell. They have been using your speech to imprison you. If you live in poverty and you say, "I'm going to be poor forever," you just created a magic spell to make you poor forever. When you see blacks on TV doing horrible crimes, it's on TV so blacks will say, "Blacks are no good," and the spell gets made. I can go down the list, but I think the point is made. Learn how to control and use your magic for yourselves and take it out of their hands. They have been using it for too long. It's easy to render them weak and useless. You can erase them from existence today if you all come together as one mentally. You all can turn blacks back to the peace-loving people who were placed here as the life of the planet. If you all come together, time will cease to exist, and you all can go back to their creation and stop it. You all control the ending. Andrew, have you ever paid attention to the plot of the story?

ANDREW: Yes, and I don't know what to believe anymore. I got the answers I was seeking, but now it feels like we're actually living the movie *Total Recall.*

IT: There you go. This is the reality you have created, and it has to play to the end. You have the villain, and you have the sleeping hero who doesn't understand his or her powers. Then you have the gods who have to intervene every so often. Blacks are depicted as the villain but are actually the hero—vice versa for the whites. As long as you accept it, it has to play until the end, or you can create your own narrative and isolate yourself from this mess. There are unlimited options for the ones with souls. This is the real black project. It's blacks' creation. As bored gods with nothing else to accomplish in the universe, you created something to occupy yourselves and something else without the use of your god powers. Andrew, my time is at the end now. All answers have been delivered. If you review and tie things together, even more answers will be revealed. It was just time for the message to be received. Any direction you choose is your choice. If you want to save your people, you have the answers; if you choose another path,

you also have the answers. You alone can change your reality. Collective action is what it would take to complete this reality or destroy it. Pay attention to your creation. You all created a foe with no soul so that, just in case he won, he loses because he dies. You all need to play it safe with this one. It's a win even if you all lose reality. Andrew, the next time I am summoned, it will be in a new reality; this one will be completed by then.

ANDREW: It, I don't know if I can't thank you enough for these revelations. I wanted answers, but now I have to do some soul-searching and try to grasp everything. Should I continue the fight in this reality, or should I just create my own? Can I turn my back on suffering? I'm lost right now, but I'll do everything as you say and turn everything into a math formula, and the solution will be the direction I choose. I can't even be angry at anyone anymore because they're just playing their roles in this reality. Thanks again, It!

IT: One more thing, Andrew. I just probed your mind, and you have to see and understand the big picture. As I stated numerous times, Farrakhan is a double agent working for both sides. The march had two meanings: one for blacks, and one for the white elites. If you stage a peaceful march, the powers always send agents in as investigators to start fights to turn the peaceful march into a brawl just to show the world that blacks can't do anything peacefully. It was noted before that this was a stimulus package to help the Washington, DC economy. The thing no one can miss is that it also let the elites know that they only need one million black men that they can control in existence to live forever. It wasn't a peaceful march as you think. It was one million black men under control. The rest of the blacks can be exterminated. The million can kill them, and one million can keep this current reality going on forever. Choose wisely, Andrew. Our choice and everyone's choice will determine the outcome. If you really comprehend the entirety of these revelations, some very powerful magic will be unlocked for you and whoever truly understands how to use it for your benefit and the benefit of your people if that's the chosen path.

ANDREW: It, please! Before you leave, I still have a few things I need answered. Why do all conscious people have the same urge to save our people?

IT: The earth's Internet is the mind. Nothing happens in secret. All the pain and suffering that happens to your people anywhere in this world is transferred to your subconscious mind every time the wind hits you. The stronger the wind is, the greater the information it brings. A very

windy day is a great information day. Understand the world you live in and how everything ties together. When the wind touches you, your brain processes and stores all the information it brings. A lot of the pain you all are feeling for your people and want revenge for is not a result of slavery; it's what's happening now across the world. You are feeling that pain and suffering, but with the lack of true understanding of what the wind brings, you attribute what you are feeling to the worst thing that ever happened in the past.

ANDREW: I think I now fully understand everything, It. Thanks again!

IT: Last thing, Andrew. Once this gets to the public, your enemies will have the same access to this information as everyone else. Do not let this be a concern to you. Just because you all have access, it doesn't mean you will have the capacity to unleash the powers that are available.

Printed in the United States
By Bookmasters